WITH ALL
THE SAINTS

WITH ALL
THE SAINTS

My Journey to the Roman Catholic Church

MARK GALLI

FOREWORD BY FRANCIS BECKWITH

Published by Word on Fire, Park Ridge, IL 60068
© 2022 by Word on Fire Catholic Ministries
Printed in the United States of America
All rights reserved.

Cover design, typesetting, and interior art direction
by Cassie Pease.

Excerpts from the English translation of the *Catechism of the Catholic Church* for
use in the United States of America Copyright © 1994, United States Catholic
Conference, Inc.—Libreria Editrice Vaticana. Used by permission. English
translation of the *Catechism of the Catholic Church*: Modifications from the Editio
Typica copyright © 1997, United States Conference of Catholic Bishops—Libreria
Editrice Vaticana.

Unless otherwise indicated, Scripture quotations are from the New Revised
Standard Version Bible: Catholic Edition (copyright © 1989, 1993), used by
permission of the National Council of the Churches of Christ in the United States
of America. All rights reserved worldwide.

24 23 22 21 1 2 3 4

ISBN: 978-1-943243-99-0

Library of Congress Control Number: 2021919684

*To my grandmother, Monica, and Uncle Ray,
who were the first to show me what everyday
Catholicism looks like.*

CONTENTS

PART III
The True Church
67

NOTES
117

FOREWORD

FRANCIS J. BECKWITH

I was born and raised Catholic, attended Catholic schools from the first through twelfth grades, and received the sacraments of Baptism, Confession, First Holy Communion, and Confirmation all before the age of thirteen. And yet, soon after my Confirmation, I found myself drawn to what seemed like the greener pastures of evangelical Christianity. It was by way of a place called Maranatha House, a small Jesus People church in downtown Las Vegas, the city in which I was raised.

I had, unbeknownst to my thirteen-year-old mind, very quickly imbibed the assumptions of my newfound evangelical friends. These assumptions included the principle of *sola scriptura* (that the Bible alone is theologically authoritative), the necessity of having a born-again experience, the importance of sharing one's faith with unbelievers (sometimes called "witnessing"), and the insignificance of the sacraments, a living Magisterium, and apostolic succession. My parents, both observant Catholics, permitted me to continue attending Maranatha House as well as several other evangelical groups. After a brief excursion into unbelief during my high school years, I returned to Christianity but not to the Catholic Church.

Although it all seems so very strange to me now, to my teenage self—a young man who just wanted to follow Jesus—the love, fellowship, and Christian commitment of my evangelical friends was attractive and over-powering. I felt like I was part of something new and special that was advancing the cause of Christ, but without the historical baggage of the Catholic Church in which I had been born. My commitment was so deep that I could not imagine my life's work being centered around anything else. For this reason, in college, I switched my major to philosophy and read just about every book I could find on theology and the Bible authored by an evangelical scholar. I was particularly smitten by works that had an apologetic flavor, that offered arguments and proofs for why it was rational to believe in God, the inerrancy and historicity of the Bible, and the truth of Christ's Resurrection.

I went on to do graduate work at an evangelical school where I studied under the Lutheran scholars John Warwick Montgomery and Charles Manske. From there, I matriculated at Fordham University, where I earned my PhD in philosophy. It was at Fordham, a Jesuit institution, that I first came in contact with serious Catholic scholars—in particular, Fr. W. Norris Clarke, SJ, and Fr. Gerald McCool, SJ—who would introduce me to the richness of Catholic philosophical thought. (Why, you may ask, would an evangelical ex-Catholic want to do advanced philosophical work at Fordham of all places? The answer: my mother, who was probably prompted by the Holy Spirit, suggested I apply there. It was as simple as that.) But my Fordham experience did not immediately draw me back to the Church, since it never occurred to me that it should. I simply saw the Catholic thinkers I had encountered—St. Augustine and St. Thomas Aquinas among them—as important and influential philosophical figures whose ideas I could appropriate to shore up my evangelical faith. It's clear to me now what I was really doing then. I was cherry-picking the tradition without realizing that everything I believed as an evangelical—all the assumptions I had imbibed—were either reactions to or deliverances of the Catholic Church that I had supposedly rejected. The Church had placed me at third base while I thought I had hit a triple. I was living off an inheritance that I was convinced I had earned. I was sitting on the shoulders of giants believing that I was standing alone. (Okay, that's too many metaphors, but you get the picture).

Over the subsequent years after Fordham—through academic appointments at UNLV, Whittier College, Trinity International University, Princeton, and finally, Baylor—I slowly began to think more and more like a Catholic, though I was not conspicuously aware of it. It was, nevertheless, so blindingly obvious to many friends and acquaintances that I was sometimes asked why I wasn't Catholic. Finally, in late April 2007, while I was serving as the fifty-eighth president of the Evangelical Theological Society, I went to confession for the first time in over thirty years. My parents, thank God, lived long enough to see me return to the Church in which they had baptized me.

While reading Mark Galli's wonderful account of his own journey to Catholicism, I found myself thinking about the evangelical world from which we both departed and what it was that ultimately carried us across the Tiber and into the Church. Because Mark and I are men of words—for we traffic in concepts, ideas, and arguments, and get paid to do it—you would think that our reversions were purely a matter of the intellect, that our choosing to become Catholic was the result of deciding which Christian group had the most intellectually persuasive case for its beliefs. There is, of course, much truth to that, as Mark carefully explains in his story. After all, one cannot help but be impressed by the Catholic Church's liturgical and doctrinal continuity with the earliest Christians, its unity and apostolicity even when enduring dissent and courting controversy, its uncanny ability to have within its ecclesial leadership both the wheat and the chaff while never abandoning the rule of faith, and its remarkable dexterity in remaining rooted in unchanging truths while faithfully addressing the theoretical challenges and practical problems endemic to every age and culture.

But that can't be the whole story. Becoming Catholic is not like buying a car, selecting a health-care plan, or picking out a pair of slacks tailored to one's specifications. It's not just a matter of weighing pros and cons and making a choice. It's more like falling in love. Yes, you have your reasons, but you are also moved by something that is not directly under your control. It took me years after returning to the Church to figure this out. I was initially under the illusion that I had made my decision exclusively as a result of successfully addressing several theological issues that I was convinced were preventing my return: the doctrine of justification, apostolic succession, the sacrament of Penance, and the doctrine of transubstantiation. But in retrospect, I now see what was really going on in my soul. I was drawn back to the Church, not merely by a compelling argument or a set of seemingly unassailable propositions, but by the whole shebang: the example of the Church's incomparable saints for two millennia; the beauty of the liturgy, even when it's done poorly; the witness of faithful friends and family over many decades; the Church's humane and realistic account of the relationship between faith and reason; its down-to-earth and nonidealistic appraisal of the human condition; its scientific, humanitarian, charitable, artistic, civilizational, and educational accomplishments; the efficacy of the sacraments and their accessibility to everyone, from the captains of industry to the cooks at the greasy diner; the fact that Dorothy Day, St. Thomas Aquinas, Kobe Bryant, Buffalo Bill Cody, St. John Henry Newman, St. Joan of Arc, Bob Newhart, St. Martin de Porres, Edith Stein, and St. Francis of Assisi can all be part of the same Church without seeming to be out of harmony with each other; *ad infinitum*. Mark Galli eloquently captures that moment when you first realize as an evangelical that you're not really qualified to interrogate the Catholic Church: "It strikes me as a sign of hubris that I would bring my lonely conscience and limited understanding and pit it against the depth and the breadth of the Church's teaching across the ages" (80).

Hubris, of course, is an equal-opportunity vice. Catholics show signs of it when they come to believe that the works and gifts of the Holy Spirit are limited only to those who are in full communion with the Church, implying that non-Catholic Christians, such as evangelicals, cannot be recipients or conduits of God's grace. The Church explicitly rejected this idea in its 1964 Decree on Ecumenism (*Unitatis Redintegratio*): "Some and even very many of the significant elements and endowments which together go to build up and give life to the Church itself, can exist outside the visible boundaries of the Catholic Church: the written word of God; the life of grace; faith, hope, and charity, with the other interior gifts of the Holy Spirit, and visible elements too. All of these, which come from Christ and lead back to Christ, belong by right to the one Church of Christ" (no. 3). As if to provide confirmation of this passage, Galli's story is teeming with evangelical friends, family members, teachers, and pastors who have truly exhibited "significant elements and endowments . . . which come from Christ and lead back to Christ." I have no doubt that it was those very aspects of evangelical life that drew me away from the Church as a young man that nevertheless helped me to keep the faith (however deficiently) for decades afterward.

Every conversion story is at bottom a love story with the same *telos*, but each one is remarkably different. Its central character can be a thief on a cross, a Roman emperor (Constantine), a North African dissatisfied with both his character and his Manichean faith (Augustine of Hippo), an agnostic Harvard undergraduate from a prominent Presbyterian family (Avery Dulles), a Polish philosopher of Jewish descent (Edith Stein), a Japanese physician who survived the atomic bomb at Nagasaki (Takashi Nagai), an ex-communist (Dorothy Day), an African-American Supreme Court justice and ex-seminarian (Clarence Thomas), or a former editor of *Christianity Today* (Galli). And what prompts them to finally embrace their newfound (or long-lost) faith can be something as simple as overhearing a neighbor's child chanting "tolle lege, tolle lege" (Augustine) or something as mysterious and mystical as being moved to tears by a Los Angeles bishop's narration of the multitudinous ways that "God uses Catholicism to utter his Word" (60).

Mark Galli's story, like each story of conversion or return, is unlike any other, and yet it is directed by the same Spirit that has for generations moved all those uneasy hearts that eventually find their rest in the barque of Peter.

August 15, 2021
Solemnity of the Assumption
of the Blessed Virgin Mary

PREFACE

As I was being swept by the current of the Tiber, my youngest daughter asked me why I was becoming a Catholic. I paused as I considered my answer, because at that moment about twelve things rushed through my mind. To give her a one- or two-sentence answer would simply misrepresent what was going on inside me. That's when it occurred to me that I may need to write a book to help not only her but especially myself understand why I had decided to become confirmed in the faith in which I was baptized as an infant.

There is, of course, another group to whom I want to explain myself: my readers. I mean those who have been kind and gracious by following my writing in *Christianity Today*, in *The Galli Report*, and in the books I've written. Many have said kind things about how my writing has helped them in one way or another, and many have said they would be interested in reading about my conversion.

I still consider myself an evangelical in some ways; there is just too much that is good and right in this tradition to simply reject it out of hand. Books by "former evangelicals" that chronicle their "liberating" move out of "oppressive" evangelicalism—well, they are dreary and, ironically, have an evangelical commitment to sharing their bad news.

I've had little personal experience with the oppressive and narrow evangelicalism of such books. There is no question that evangelicalism has flaws, some rather serious. And to be sure, I've formally left that movement in one sense; I've now been confirmed in the Roman Catholic Church. But to the degree that I've left, I've left without bitterness.

In the course of this book, I tell stories, I make arguments, I explain doctrines, I "commit psychology" here and there. After all that—and after cutting out large sections of the first draft—my heart, mind, and motivations remain, alas, a mystery to me. I suspect I'll never fully understand, or be able to explain from a human perspective, why I've made this move.

But it's a start.

ACKNOWLEDGMENTS

Among the people who have encouraged me in my journey, let me mention just a few.

Theresa Galli, the daughter who asked me an innocent question about the reason for my conversion, which made me realize I couldn't answer with a simple sentence.

Adam Stevenson, educator, friend, and now fellow Catholic, who helped me think more clearly as I was making my way down the Tiber.

Ben Lovaasen, chemistry professor, friend, and convinced Lutheran in theology, who did the same.

Jay Wood, professor of theology, friend, and faithful Anglican, who also did the same.

John Seaborn, theologian from the Augustine Institute in Denver, who helped me unravel some of my confusion about things Catholic.

Michael Galli, a faithful brother, who took the time to read and comment on the not-so-readable first draft of the book.

Bishop Robert Barron, who, as I was taking baby steps toward Catholicism, gave good advice during a pivotal phone conversation.

Fathers Dan Hoehn and Max Behna at St. Michael's in Wheaton, who have provided wise pastoral guidance in the confessional and from the pulpit.

Word on Fire editors Brandon Vogt, Matthew Becklo, Daniel Seseske, Lauren Mann, and Danny O'Brien who helped bring the manuscript to the light of day.

Barbara, my wife of forty-seven years, who has the annoying gift of being absolutely honest about my writing, and who has never complained about and has even enabled my addiction to writing, even as this solitary pursuit has often interfered with family responsibilities.

This is a better book because of how these and others have been kind in their critiques and generous with their encouragement. Alas, they cannot be held responsible for any advice they gave that I ignored.

PART I

Tributaries

CHAPTER 1

It's about Jesus:
Evangelicalism

Conversion—it's complicated. We find ourselves changed but not exactly sure how it happened. Sometimes it's not clear what we are being converted from or converted to. A conversion to Catholicism does not necessarily begin with a conscious awareness that Catholicism is where one is headed. God is more subtle.

One can confuse a tributary for the main river into which it feeds. If the main river is substantial, the tributaries will be as well. Only when you find yourself merging into the main river do you realize you've been in a tributary. The traditional metaphor for becoming Catholic is "crossing the Tiber"—a reference to the river that runs through the city of Rome. If you approach the Vatican from the east, you literally have to cross the Tiber to get there. A better metaphor for my journey would not be that I crossed the Tiber but that I let myself be carried on it toward Vatican City, where I knew I was to get off.

Until then, I had dropped my boat into tributaries that I believed would lead me home. I discovered that they all ended up in the same place: a river called Tiber. I've traveled at least three tributaries, maybe four, which more precisely might be called conversions.

⁊

I begin with the most crucial conversion. Unfortunately, I have no memory of it. Since I'm trying to discern the conscious reasons for my affiliation with Rome, I'll have to bracket it. But theologically, it's decisive.

It happened in 1952 at St. Gabriel's Catholic Church in San Francisco a little more than a month after my birth. I was baptized, which in Catholic theology is definitely a conversion—from a state of original sin to a state of grace. One would wish that such a conversion would be memorable, but alas, this is one downside to infant Baptism.

Apparently, it didn't mean a whole lot to my family, since I don't recall attending church as a boy—until it came time to receive First Communion. I vaguely remember catechism classes to prepare for that, though I remember nothing I was taught. I do remember that my younger brother deeply impressed the sisters with his apparent devotion. (As these things go, he became the prodigal, and I the minister.) I also have a memory of going to confession and afterward kneeling in a pew and saying a number of Hail Marys and Our Fathers in penance—I assume in preparation for receiving First Communion. To be frank, I don't know that I would remember First Communion except for the family pictures of me and my brother in coats and ties, Grandma Galli in a flowered dress, and my mother in a stunning white suit with her black hair piled dramatically high.

Since we didn't start attending church after that, I've gathered that the reason for these two sacraments was my Catholic paternal grandmother, who I suspect nagged my father into forcing the issue, maybe with a refrain I heard often as a child: "Now, Bob . . ." Overall during childhood, religion was simply absent from my consciousness. One might argue, when listening to other stories of Catholic upbringing, that this void of Catholicism is what made for the complete happiness of those years!

All to say, it wasn't until my first conscious conversion that God became more than a swear word to me. It culminated at an altar call at the Evangelical Free Church of Felton, California, in December 1965, when I was thirteen years old.

⁊

A few months earlier, my mother had given her life to Christ. She had a rocky relationship with my older brother, Michael, as he began to enter adulthood at the end of high school and into his first year at community college. Since he lived at home, my mother's need for psychological control and my brother's need for independence often exploded into shouting matches and slammed doors. After one intense bout that led to my brother bolting from the house (with the characteristic slammed door), my mother prayed in desperation, "Lord, if you get Michael to join the army, I'll accept Jesus."

The groundwork for that prayer had been laid for months, as her sister, Sasha, a devout and annoying evangelical, had been witnessing to her about Jesus. It apparently brought a glint of clarity in my mother's otherwise confused heart, and in a crisis, she blurted out what amounted to a bargain with the Master of the Universe. She had no idea with whom she was dealing. Later that day, my brother returned home and announced that he had joined the Air Force. To my mother's mind, that was close enough, and a deal was a deal.

Some weeks later, she tuned in to a Billy Graham crusade broadcast on a local TV station. During the altar call, with the choir singing "Just As I Am" in the background, Graham turned to the camera and said that those at home who wanted to receive Jesus as their Lord and Savior could do so by kneeling in front of their televisions and praying the sinner's prayer along with him. My mother went to her knees.

When my mother found a new passion, the rest of the family (except for my father) was afflicted with it as well. Soon after the fateful deal, my older brother left for the Air Force, and we moved to Aptos, California. As my mom's religious enthusiasm caught hold, the family included my brother Steven (not yet a prodigal), my cousin Judy (who was separated from her husband, pregnant, and living with us at the time), and me. We were cajoled not only into attending Sunday morning worship and Sunday school but also Sunday evening worship and Wednesday night prayer meetings at the Evangelical Free Church of Felton.

The pastor—really the church in general—had so emphasized the need to be "grounded in the Word" that my mom thought we should study the

Bible together every night we were not at church. She naïvely assumed that this was the habit of all Christians. So, after the dishes were cleared, we'd bring our Bibles to the table and work our way through the Gospel of John. At first, none of us had Bibles to speak of, so we had scrounged them up wherever we could find them. My mom found one for me at a flea market—a King James Version she picked up for fifty cents.

Cigarette smoke swirled around my mom's coffee cup and Bible as we explored "the strange new world within the Bible," as Karl Barth put it. Naturally, Barth was unknown to us, but the power of the Bible to reorient us was becoming a new if strange reality every night.

What was cemented in heart and mind during that period took place in one Sunday school class. The teacher read some passage in which Jesus had commanded something of his disciples—the particular passage has long left my memory. He asked the class of restless junior high kids, "Why should we do what Jesus tells us to do in this passage?" Various answers came forth, all of which amounted to one version of pragmatism or another: it would be good for us, it would be good for others, and so forth. The teacher kept shaking his head, saying, "Those things may be true, but those are not the main reason we should obey this command." When we finally admitted we were stumped, the teacher said, "We obey this command because it was given by Jesus."

Even at age thirteen, I marveled at the wisdom of this simple answer. For reasons too mysterious and complex to fathom, this has become an unshakable conviction for me ever since. We obey the teachings of Jesus, and of Scripture in general, because of their divine origin. Today, I recognize how difficult it is sometimes to hear the voice of the Lord in Scripture or in prayer, as well as how nuanced and varied our interpretations of what that voice is saying can be. But between those evening Bible studies and the insight of my Sunday school teacher, I've never been able to seriously doubt that the Bible is the Word of God or that Jesus is the focal point of Scripture and thus, naturally, the Word of God in a deeper sense. To be clear, it would be a number of years before I *loved* the Bible, but more on that in a bit—one conversion at a time.

Among the other things I imbibed at this fundamentalist church was the need to make a "public profession of faith." Specifically, that meant the need to come forward during an altar call and accept Jesus as Lord and Savior, either committing or recommitting one's life to Christ. Altar calls were a fixed liturgical feature in the Sunday morning service, with every sermon ending with one; however, there was rarely a call to stand up and walk the aisle forward. Instead—usually with every head bowed and eyes shut—Pastor Lawrence would ask anyone who wanted to make a commitment to raise a hand.

Sometimes, if there were no takers, he would broaden the appeal and ask people to raise their hands if they were burdened by some sin; if there were still no takers, he would start naming particular sins. My mother—whose checkered history included three marriages, giving up a baby daughter, and long battles with alcohol and depression—still had a lot of worldly wit in her, and would joke that sometimes Pastor Lawrence was so desperate for a raised hand that she was sure he was going to say, "Tennis anyone?"

She was also usually desperate for a smoke after worship, so while everyone gathered for coffee in the narthex, she'd go out to the parking lot and light up. Needless to say, smoking was considered a sin in this church. But I give credit to the pastor and members, who never criticized her for smoking, with one elderly man regularly taking the trouble to leave coffee fellowship to come and talk to my mom in the parking lot. I've read many accounts of people who have had horrific, manipulative, and abusive relationships in their fundamentalist churches. Though I don't deny their experiences, I've never been able to relate, as my experience of this church was affirming, even though I've come to reject some of its teachings and practices.

In retrospect, I've realized that Pastor Lawrence was a master of the altar call. Every Sunday, guilt and uncertainty would course through me as he invited unbelievers to raise their hand. After enduring this for months, and as Christmas was approaching, I'd had enough of this spiritual dread. I decided to raise my hand at the end of the service the Sunday before Christmas. I didn't want to feel guilty any longer.

So on December 19, 1965, I entered the A-frame sanctuary and slid into a shiny wooden pew next to my mom, my brother, and my cousin, as was our routine. When Pastor Lawrence asked those who wanted to receive Jesus into their lives to raise their hands, mine shot up immediately. That's when Pastor Lawrence pulled a fast one. I'd been attending for months, and never in all that time did he ask people to stand up and come forward. So when he asked all those who raised their hand to come forward and pray with one of the elders, I was annoyed. This was not what I had bargained for. But I had made a commitment by raising my hand, so forward I went.

An older man escorted me to the bride's room, and we knelt and put our elbows on two metal folding chairs. He led me through the sinner's prayer line by line. We had to pause a couple of times because I was crying so hard. I wasn't mature enough to grasp the enormity of my sin and the utter graciousness of Jesus, so I don't think this was in play. I'm sure the anxiety and guilt produced by many home Bible studies and weekly church services was what burst forth as I prayed.

A month later, I was baptized by immersion. For a long time, I considered this my real baptism. Then for a time, I'd joke that I was well-covered, since I'd been baptized by sprinkling as an infant in the Roman Catholic Church and by full immersion as an adult (or at least at the age of accountability) in a Protestant church. Of course, I now celebrate my Baptism every September 28, the day I was baptized in 1952 at St. Gabriel's Catholic Church. But at the time, discipled as I was in evangelical religion, baptism was not the real marker. I believed I had been saved on December 19, 1965, at about noon. This is the sort of thing evangelicals do: we know the day and hour of our conversion, when we were set up to enjoy eternal life.

And yet immediately there were complications. In particular, the next Sunday, the day after Christmas, I again went to church with the family, and as Pastor Lawrence warmed up to the altar call, I was shocked to discover I felt just as guilty as ever! What the heck? Another thing I hadn't bargained for. But I remembered the words of the elder with whom I had prayed, who had assured me that once I had confessed Christ with my lips, I was saved.

This was the first inkling that the Christian life was not as simple as I had imagined. This was also the moment when I realized—though I couldn't have articulated it like this—that human psychology was in play in the religious life.

I soon learned that altar calls were part and parcel of the fundamentalist liturgical year. The church sponsored an annual missions week as well as an annual revival, both of which were opportunities "to get right with the Lord." This revealed to me the inherent paradox of this tradition: On the one hand, it was declared that once you accepted Jesus as Lord and Savior, it was a done deal. You were assured of the forgiveness of sins and entry into eternal life. But every revival preacher was skilled at making you doubt your original profession of faith or convincing you that you had backslidden. Thus, many believers shared the experience of one of my young friends at the church: one day he told me that he had already accepted Jesus six or seven times. Though mightily tempted to go forward during the altar call at times, I never did so again; I kept telling myself, *I've already done that!*

I've concluded, years later, that the weekly altar calls and the annual revivals were the fundamentalist version of the Eucharist—regular events where one goes forth bodily to receive the grace of God in fresh ways. "Once saved, always saved" has a lot going for it theologically, but weak human beings need to participate bodily in their salvation and do so regularly. As much as the fundamentalists wanted to get away from anything that smacked of Catholicism, they couldn't escape the fundamental truth of Catholicism: the body matters, as does liturgy. Apparently, neither could I.

This conversion, then, was a conversion to Jesus at a basic level. Along with it came a deep respect for Scripture, the need for daily prayer, and the willingness to live my life as a Christian. This planted me in the tributary of evangelical Christianity, whose twists and turns and rapids I navigated for fifty years. I won't detail all of them but only the ones that left their mark on me.

CHAPTER 2

Mind-Expanding Faith:
Theology

It would be fair to say that my early faith was more or less shaped by a sense of duty. I had made a commitment, and I was responsible to act on it. If you get the impression that I was a "good boy" and never went through a rebellious period in my teen years, you'd be more or less right. To be clear, this religious activity wasn't an unpleasant duty. There were so many things to learn and so many things to challenge me. There is duty that is drudgery, and then there is duty like that of first responders; religious duty can be intriguing, exciting, and sometimes life-threatening. Life-threatening to a teenager anyway.

Somewhere in those early years, my mom became attracted to Bill Bright's Campus Crusade evangelistic method. My mother being my mother was not satisfied that she had drawn her boys and niece into the faith; so excited was she about how Jesus changed her own life, she was on the lookout for ways to share her faith with anyone and everyone. She once painted our galvanized garbage can black and put colorful butterfly decals on it. She was hoping it would catch the attention of the garbageman, who might ask her about it. She would then, of course, talk about the butterfly as a symbol of the Resurrection, which would segue into her testimony. I don't remember if that ever happened, but we did have the most amazing garbage can on our street.

When Bill Bright was passing through the Santa Cruz area to talk about his Four Spiritual Laws, my mom decided we should all attend his talk. Soon we were trained in the method, driven to the beach in front of the Santa Cruz Boardwalk, and sent forth to evangelize. Well, at least to ask people to take a religious survey. I don't remember any of the questions but the last. The question previous to that must have been about the assurance of forgiveness and eternal life, because the next question we were to ask was, "Would you like to hear more about how you can experience the forgiveness of sins and the assurance of eternal life?" If the person said yes, cue *The Four Spiritual Laws*, Bill Bright's highly condensed version of the Gospel. Heart beating wildly, I went forth, found a woman, and went through the drill. But there was no interest in hearing more about forgiveness. I'm not sure how many people I approached/annoyed that day, but I'm sure that I didn't create a single convert. I certainly don't recall sharing *The Four Spiritual Laws* with anyone.

The truly life-threatening moment came soon afterward when I decided to phone a girl I had a crush on. I would begin with the survey, share the Laws, and then she'd become a Christian—as well as my girlfriend. These thoughts were unformed, to be sure, but I suspect they moved in this direction. Well, with a fair amount of nervousness and trepidation, I dialed her, and she happily agreed to take the survey, which led to *The Four Spiritual Laws*, which led to a decided "no"—she didn't want to receive Christ into her life.

I was crushed, and trudged upstairs to tell my mom and her Christian friend what had happened. Her friend assured me (with a kindly face that I often saw in my mother's fundamentalist friends) that I had nonetheless planted a seed, and that was a good thing. This brought some comfort, but honestly not much. It quickly occurred to me that I was now going to be cast out from the cool circle in which this girl moved. For a teenager, that was the equivalent of death. But I held steady because this was the price of being a Christian. I was supposed to share my faith with others. That's what a Christian did, even if it meant rejection by some.

Day to day, though, my faith usually amounted to trying not to sin—a losing proposition if there ever was one. By God's grace, that changed after a conversation with an older friend. By this time, our family (sans Dad) had started attending First Presbyterian Church of Santa Cruz. I can't remember the reasons for the switch. Perhaps my mother was tired of the twenty-five-minute drive to the church in Felton, or perhaps the fundamentalism was becoming a bit oppressive for her free spirit. It may very well have been that there was a good youth group for me and my brother at "First Pres."

At any rate, I happily participated in the youth group, and one day, one of the leaders, Kent, bumped into me and began asking questions about what was going on. He not only asked about my life; he actually looked like he was interested in what I had to say. Somehow this little encounter turned a light on. I understood for the first time that being a Christian wasn't about obeying an increasingly long list of rules but about loving one's neighbor. I chalk this up to a gift of the Holy Spirit, but I won't argue with anyone who says this was merely a natural psychological development for a young person, maturing from a rule-based life to one focused on relationships. I'm not convinced one has to choose between explanations. One has to ask who created human beings so that they would move in this psychological direction. God is not averse to using human psychology.

Yet I was still pretty immature, because now love became an overarching duty! If I loved God and neighbor, wouldn't I do this or that or still another thing? Specifically, wouldn't I want to become a leader in the youth group and then the college group, and join the choir as well as the youth choir's production of *Godspell*, and act in the church's theater group, and, and, and. The one thing I can say for this period is that it spoke volumes of my endurance, as I didn't become exhausted for three or four years. But eventually, I fell apart. It wasn't a classic breakdown with tears or collapse into a catatonic state. It was more a deep weariness and nagging doubt. I was busy with all this activity because, among other things, I had determined during this frenetic period that I was going to become a pastor. After all, if I loved God, wasn't this one of the best ways to love my neighbor? Perhaps becoming a missionary would demonstrate more ardor, but for whatever reason, pastoral ministry seemed good enough.

But as I entered the last stage of my exhaustion, it occurred to me that I had never really prayed about becoming a pastor; I never had asked God if this was something he wanted me to do. It was just my own grand idea, which of course was only praised and honored by the Christian adults to whom I mentioned it. To a young man, such affirmation is a drug, and I happily lived on the high it gave me. But it occurred to me that maybe God didn't want me to be a pastor. This of course shook me, since I had made this the cornerstone of my identity. I soon concluded—again, I suppose out of a sense of duty—that I had no business presuming on the will of God in this matter. In fact, I decided I needed a long sabbatical to think and pray about all this. So I dropped every responsibility I had taken up, to the disappointment of many people who had been counting on me. But never mind; I had to get this business straightened out. I determined not to volunteer for any leadership position until it was clear that God was calling me to do so.

It was during that sabbatical that my second conversion occurred.

೦೨

This conversion cannot be neatly dated. It took place over a period of months, in the winter and spring quarters of my junior year at the University of California at Santa Cruz. For that reason, I have a hard time remembering events that triggered this conversion.

Though I had stepped away from leadership, I still participated in worship and Bible studies at church. I assume that I continued to have morning "quiet times"—evangelical lingo for prayer and Bible reading—but I honestly don't remember. What I do remember is that during those months, I began to love reading the Bible. I became fascinated with it. I found myself reading it and taking notes at all hours of the day. Before this, I was a regular reader of Scripture, but I read it out of a sense of duty—and again, not duty as drudgery. But it also was not a delight. I didn't love reading and pondering the meaning of the Bible. I never had keen insights or "ah ha" moments when I read it. I didn't seem to have the ability to penetrate its depth, as did my friend Bill.

Bill was an amazing presence at the weekly Seekers meeting—the college group at First Pres—where we studied the Bible together. Bill would say very

13

little as the rest of us spouted one opinion or another, or argued with one another about the meaning of the text. Toward the end of the discussion, Bill would weigh in, "It seems to me . . ." He spoke in a way that never put anyone else down; he just articulated his view of the passage at hand in a matter-of-fact way. But what he had to say was usually insightful, and it made the previous discussion seem trivial. I, at least, was always amazed, and it made me recognize that I didn't read the Bible as Bill did. I didn't envy him or aspire to be like him (well, *mostly* didn't). I just noted that the Bible didn't intrigue or interest me like that.

But over the winter and spring quarters, it did. I became ravenous for Scripture. I was in a class on modern theology—Karl Barth, Martin Buber, Rudolf Bultmann, and the like—and I found myself suddenly fascinated with theology. I became enamored with Barth's *Epistle to the Romans*, though I understood very little of it. I started reading Romans myself and kept a journal with my own commentary. I began having insights into the text that, on a good day, matched those of my friend Bill. I should make clear that my new love of Scripture was almost purely intellectual. I was eating up the Bible as a source of theology, not necessarily moral guidance. I didn't ignore its moral teaching and followed it as much as any immature college student is able. But it was theology that captivated me.

This conversion fanned the flames of a desire to teach the Bible and its theology. This left me in a bind, of course, because I had vowed to not become a leader in any capacity until I felt a definite sense of call. And so I stuck to my vow, deciding that such Scripture study would for me be a personal passion. During this period, I had begun to attend another college group Bible study, which met weekly at Merrill College at UCSC. The university was structured like some British universities, with a number of colleges that each had its own specialty. And at each college, there was a weekly Bible study for the Christians who lived there. The larger conservative Christian fellowship, composed of all the college groups, would meet once a month.

UCSC was progressive, to say the least. During the 1972 presidential election, 96 percent of the students voted for the far-left Democrat George

McGovern, while only a handful voted for Richard Nixon; the rest checked off the socialist candidate on their ballot. Students participated in their fair share of protests against the Vietnam War, blocking traffic on the highway that led into Santa Cruz and creating havoc downtown, after which a few friends in the college group who joined the protest found themselves in jail for a few hours. It was a time when professors would sometimes hold their classes outdoors in the amphitheater, in the midst of a grove of redwoods. In that natural setting, with the spring sun warming things up all around, one or two coeds would remove their tops. We undergrad men tried desperately to act like it was nothing.

It was also a student body that was more or less hostile to Christianity, as this religion was part of "the establishment," which was seen as nothing but bad. We were sometimes publicly mocked for our beliefs, some of which were shocking to some students. I recall sitting by the library reading one afternoon when I overheard two coeds talking about the Crucifixion, exclaiming how sick it was that Christians spent so much time talking about that horrid event. Of course, they were right; they grasped how shocking and grotesque a crucifixion is, and how absurd it would be to found a faith upon it. Which is why evangelistic conversations at UCSC could be so interesting. We encouraged such conversations in a variety of ways.

For example, at the beginning of the year, we set up a book table full of Christian literature. This led to conversations, sometimes to arguments—and occasionally also to shock. One professor happened by and was genuinely curious about the books on the table—until he recognized they were books about Christian faith. Then a look of horror crossed his face, and he slowly backed away, as if he would catch a disease. Another strategy was to offer "Ask Christians Anything" wine and cheese sessions in the dorm. The wine, of course, was the attraction, and a way to show our dormmates we were down with alcohol and all that. And indeed, some lively conversations about Jesus were had. So anxious were we Christians to be cool that a couple of the Christians at one meeting imbibed a little too much wine in the course of the evangelistic conversation, and within an hour or so, found themselves drunk and vomiting in the hallway. Not exactly the Christian witness we were aiming for.

At any rate, I began attending the weekly Bible study at Merrill College and participating in the conversations. This is also where I met Barbara, the woman who was to become my wife—though we to this day disagree about the exact encounter that started us paying attention to one another. All I can say at this point is that I am right. Kidding aside, I bring this up to be frank about what was going on in another part of my heart at the time: I was falling in love. This was complicated, because I already had a fiancée, who attended another California college. But it was Barbara who was becoming a friend in a way that this other woman was not. My fiancée was an extraordinary woman—a thoughtful, kind, and devout Christian—and I loved her because of that and more. But I discovered in our time apart, and in meeting Barbara, that she wasn't really a friend, someone who shared some deeper interests with me. Eventually, this led to the breakup with my fiancée, and more eventually still to my engagement and marriage to Barbara.

This was happening during the same period when my love of Scripture and Christian theology was enflamed, and no, I cannot deny that they each fed into each other, especially since Barbara was taking that class in modern theology with me, and we wrote our term paper together. That God would use romantic love as a pathway into spiritual love—this is not a new tactic of the Almighty, devious as it is. Yet in my mind they were parallel tracks that really had nothing to do with one another—happy coincidences. But I was naïve in this.

At the end of the spring semester, the leader of the group pulled me aside one day. It was his senior year, and he was about to graduate. He said, "I think you should lead the Bible studies next year." He proceeded to tell me all the reasons, one of them being my deep love of Scripture. I said I'd pray about it—a standard evangelical reply. I then talked to a couple of close friends in the group, including Barbara, all of whom agreed I should do it. Long story short, I took this as confirmation of a divine call—not only to lead this Bible study but to continue to pursue becoming a minister. One can never be sure of one's real motives in doing anything. As I look back, I can see a great deal of pride mixed with a desire to preach and teach the Bible. But I'm nonetheless convinced this was a divine call to teach, a call I have responded to my whole life, through both my work as a preacher and teacher in congregations as well as through my writing, which I have always considered a mode of teaching.

This was a long and enjoyable tributary on which to travel. One might call it the tributary of truth—meaning both the search for and the teaching of the truth of the Gospel. I've had a lifelong love affair with Scripture and theology in which I've tried to penetrate the mystery and wonder of the Christian faith and then communicate that to listeners and readers. To be sure, this led to a fair amount of pride and self-righteous indignation, especially when I believed that other Christians had gotten this or that wrong.

The old joke applies here: when the World Wide Web first attracted general interest, a cartoon appeared in which a young man is telling his wife, "I'll come to bed in just a moment. I have to see if anyone said something wrong on the internet." I'm afraid that characterized too much of my theological interest for too long. And yet the Lord was patient with me, and he used my reading of theology to carry me to the Tiber.

CHAPTER 3

Dipping My Toes in the Tiber

In my journey on the evangelical and theological tributaries, there were brief moments when it occurred to me that they may have been leading me to the Tiber.

For example, I recall as a Presbyterian minister in Sacramento in the early 1990s attending morning Mass and buying a *St. Joseph Sunday Missal* to guide my personal prayers. It was clear that I was already looking for something more than everyday evangelicalism or Presbyterianism. But that was a phase that soon petered out when it became clear I couldn't receive Communion at Mass, and when I could not make head nor tails of how to use the missal.

If I were to pick one moment above others, it was years later, when I sat in bed reading *The Splendor of Truth*, the 1993 encyclical by John Paul II. I don't remember what prompted me to order and read this, though I remember being fascinated (as were millions of others at the time) with this pope. At any rate, it became clear in a few pages that it was a comprehensive philosophical guide to Catholic moral theology. Night after night, as I chewed on a few pages at a time, I marveled at its wisdom. It is a patient, thoughtful, and wise work, grounded in Scripture and Catholic moral theology while engaging contemporary philosophy. It begins and ends with the story of the rich young ruler as a paradigm and is driven by sensitive pastoral concern throughout. John Paul II concludes,

> In the heart of every Christian, in the inmost depths of each person, there is always an echo of the question which the young man in the Gospel once asked Jesus, "Teacher, what good must I do to have eternal life?"

(Matt. 19:16). Everyone, however, needs to address this question to the "Good Teacher," since he is the only one who can answer in the fullness of truth, in all situations, in the most varied of circumstances. And when Christians ask him the question which rises from their conscience, the Lord replies in the words of the New Covenant which have been entrusted to his Church. As the Apostle Paul said of himself, we have been sent to "preach the Gospel, and not with eloquent wisdom, lest the Cross of Christ be emptied of its power" (1 Cor. 1:17). The Church's answer to man's question contains the wisdom and power of Christ Crucified, the Truth which gives of itself.

At the time, I was editor of the magazine *Christian History*, a part of the family of magazines at *Christianity Today*. It was a leisurely quarterly, with a theme topic or person for each issue, from "Worship in the Early Church" to "John Chrysostom" to "Martin Luther" to "The Great Awakening." As I was reading *Veritatis Splendor*, I was editing the issue on Francis of Assisi. If I marveled at the intellect of John Paul II, I also was moved by the astounding devotion of Francis in following Jesus as literally as he knew how, which meant for him a life of absolute poverty.

And then there were the Francis stories. Even if some turned out to be mere legends, they spoke volumes about how Francis impressed people of his day—from the kissing of lepers, whom he had previously abhorred, to giving away his cloak in the middle of winter to a shivering sojourner, to preaching to the birds, to the taming of the wolf of Gubbio. But there are lesser-known stories that also left a deep impression on me, like one from a fourteenth-century manuscript in which Francis explains to his companion Brother Leo "what true joy is."

"A messenger comes and says that all the masters of theology in Paris have joined the Order . . . that is not true joy," says Francis. "Or all the prelates beyond the mountains—archbishops and bishops, or the King of France and the King of England . . . that is not true joy." He goes on with more examples, including mass conversions of unbelievers and healings and miracles. "I tell you," he says, "that true joy is not in all those things." When asked by Brother Leo, "But what is true joy?" he replies,

> "I am returning from Perugia, and I am coming here at night, in the dark. It is winter time and wet and muddy and so cold that icicles form at the edges of my habit and keep striking my legs, and blood flows from such wounds. And I come to the gate, all covered in mud and cold and ice, and after I have knocked and called for a long time, a friar comes and asks, 'Who are you?' I answer, 'Brother Francis.' And he says, 'Go away. This is not a decent time to be going about. You can't come in.'"

Francis imagines insisting on being let in, and the friar says, "Go away! You are a simple and uneducated fellow. . . . We are so many and so important that we don't need you."

But Francis still imagines himself at the gate, saying, "For the love of God, let me come in tonight!" To which the friar answers, "I won't. Go to the lepers' hospital and ask there." Francis concludes to Brother Leo: "I tell you that if I kept patience and was not upset—that is true joy and true virtue and salvation of the soul."

I edited the Francis issue by day and read *The Splendor of Truth* by night, and one evening, I sat amazed that the same Church had produced both men—one a man that stirred within me both wonder and joy, and another with extraordinary intellectual gifts and pastoral sensitivity.

That was the moment I started flirting with Catholicism.

I recall a conversation with a friend who had recently converted, and she was insistent that I know that, contra the longings of conservative evangelicals for a Magisterium (and thus a key motive in many evangelical conversions), there were many dissenting voices on the Catholic left. She assured me that not everyone agreed with the Magisterium. This struck me as an odd thing to tell someone who was thinking about becoming Catholic. Her speech made me think she was still a Protestant at heart. What's the point of becoming a Catholic if you are immediately going to join with those who are trying to sabotage ecclesial and biblical authority very much along the lines of liberal Protestantism, all in the quest to be relevant, to accommodate modernity? Why not just stay Protestant?

I've seen the same tendency in circles of extreme conservative Catholics, many of whom have come out of evangelicalism. They become Catholic because they believe it will be hard to budge the Church from its moral, theological, and structural traditions; the attraction to Catholicism, it appears, is in its apparent conservatism. So when a Pope Francis comes along and makes environmental health a major concern, they act like the vault of St. Peter's Basilica is falling. They create all manner of conspiracy theories, including questions about the legitimacy of Vatican II: "The liberals are on the verge of taking over and destroying the Church!" Again, Protestantism, but colored conservative.

Even at this stage it was apparent to me that to become Catholic would mean embracing the Church and its doctrines, ethics, councils, and hierarchy—not in the spirit of an abject subservience that never questions, but in joyful and free obedience to something greater than one's self; not for the sake of obedience as such, but because one is convinced this is the true Church. Of course, there is room for disagreement and debate, which has been good for the Church, as its history attests time and again. But to question not just the opinions but the very legitimacy of councils and popes that one disagrees with—that struck me as simply being Protestant while wearing the trappings of Catholicism.

At any rate, at this point in my career, moving into Catholicism was not an option. By this time, I was managing editor of *Christianity Today*, which was founded by Billy Graham and is arguably the leading voice of mainstream evangelicalism in the US if not the world. I was soon to become editor in chief of this venerable evangelical publication. I knew that to become a Catholic would mean losing my job. And yet that was not an issue for me; something deeper was.

At this point, I had earned enough professional respect that I could have found respectable editorial work in a variety of outlets where Catholicism

21

wouldn't be an issue. But every time I began to explore other career options, I found myself deeply unsettled and came to believe that this was the stirring of the Holy Spirit for me to stay put at CT. Decades before, I believed I had been called out of pastoral ministry to work in Christian journalism, and I still felt that I was called specifically to CT. I didn't know exactly why, nor for how long the Lord would require my services there, but it seemed clear to me that I was not permitted to leave anytime soon. I would know when I was free to go, I concluded, just as I had known at other key junctures of my life it was time to move on.

Furthermore, I understood that my job at CT was to promote the best of evangelical Christianity. It was by no means a perfect movement. There were even some lines in CT's statement of faith with which I disagreed. But especially as editor in chief, it was not my duty to foist my increasingly Catholic (and sometime Orthodox) beliefs on our readers, but rather to oversee a staff that would produce the best evangelical reporting and commentary.

This put me in some awkward situations from time to time, especially when as editor in chief I had to publicly defend some cardinal point of CT's theology I questioned. I quickly discerned the way to handle such matters: I would talk about what evangelicals or CT believed, as well as the reasons for that belief. But I wouldn't lie; I wouldn't use the first-person pronoun to suggest that I personally believed it. My responsibility as editor in chief was, again, not to foist my personal beliefs on readers but to represent the magazine and what it stood for in the larger world of evangelicalism.

And yet it was clear that evangelical religion as such was not sufficient for me. Because I respected the movement and the tradition, I could in good faith happily edit a magazine that promoted its cause. It exalts Jesus, his Crucifixion and Resurrection, the authority of Scripture, and the need to spread the Gospel in word and deed—what's not to admire? But it didn't satisfy what I was yearning for, partly because I wasn't even sure what that was yet.

So, during this period, becoming a Catholic had no purchase on my imagination, even though I found it deeply attractive in many ways. I was, at it were, flowing inevitably into the Tiber. I was searching for something more, something deeper, something more transcendent. And just when my little boat was about to merge into the Tiber, I rowed ashore and got out, looking for yet another way.

CHAPTER 4

The Gateway Tradition:
Anglicanism

Like many, my initial attraction to Anglicanism came through the *Book of Common Prayer*. As a good evangelical, I consistently strove to have my daily "quiet time"—the reading of Scripture and prayer each morning. This was a spiritual discipline I picked up in high school and continued through college, seminary, and pastoral ministry. It was during my stint as pastor of Grace Presbyterian Church in Sacramento, California, that I began to seriously weary of this practice.

Reading the Bible was still as engaging as ever, but I was increasingly dissatisfied with my prayer life. It seemed so paltry. Here I was addressing the Creator of the universe in words pedestrian and boring. I grant that God listens attentively to the gibberish of even small children, but it struck me that a literate adult with a master's degree should be able to do something more than babble in the presence of the Almighty. This was not only because God deserved the best language I could offer, but also because the words that came tumbling out of my mouth rarely if ever expressed what was going on inside me. It was babel, plain and simple.

I can't remember the occasion when I stumbled upon the *Book of Common Prayer*, but when I did, it was—excuse the expression—a godsend. After figuring out how to navigate the book (no small feat), I discovered prayers that startled me for their beauty and brevity, and especially their ability to say exactly what I was thinking and feeling. I soon moved from offering weak and meager confessions ("I'm sorry Lord that I said this and did that") to memorizing prayers like this:

Most merciful God,
we confess that we have sinned against you
in thought, word, and deed,
by what we have done,
and by what we have left undone.
We have not loved you with our whole heart;
we have not loved our neighbors as ourselves.
We are truly sorry and we humbly repent.
For the sake of your Son Jesus Christ,
have mercy on us and forgive us;
that we may delight in your will,
and walk in your ways,
to the glory of your Name. Amen.

And from "I just thank you Lord for this, that, and the other thing, and help me to serve you today," I began praying prayers like this:

Almighty God, Father of all mercies,
we your unworthy servants give you humble thanks
for all your goodness and loving-kindness
to us and to all whom you have made.
We bless you for our creation, preservation,
and all the blessings of this life;
but above all for your immeasurable love
in the redemption of the world by our Lord Jesus Christ;
for the means of grace, and for the hope of glory.
And, we pray, give us such an awareness of your mercies,
that with truly thankful hearts we may show forth your praise,
not only with our lips, but in our lives,
by giving up our selves to your service,
and by walking before you
in holiness and righteousness all our days;

through Jesus Christ our Lord,

to whom, with you and the Holy Spirit,

be honor and glory throughout all ages. Amen.

So I began reciting the daily office—well, at least morning prayer—as many days as I could. In the summer of 1989, our family moved to the western suburbs of Chicago so that I could take up the position of associate editor at *Leadership Journal*. Since I was an ordained Presbyterian minister, it was only natural to seek out a local Presbyterian church to attend. For a few Sundays we tried this Presbyterian church and that, but nothing clicked. Then one Sunday, as my wife and three children lay sick in bed, I decided to visit the local Episcopal church, Saint Mark's in Glen Ellyn. My reasoning was simple: if I enjoyed the *Book of Common Prayer* so much, perhaps I would also find the Sunday liturgy equally fulfilling.

I was wrong. I found it extraordinary. For the first six Sundays that I attended the church, I wept during the Eucharist. It was not just the beauty and cadence of the liturgy, but especially what took place during the Eucharist. What struck me was how rich and poor, old and young, men and women and boys and girls, rose from their seats, stood in line, and knelt humbly at the communion rail to partake of the bread and wine. But what sealed the deal that first Sunday was a dear soul, Lois Baker, who gave each visitor a fresh-baked loaf of bread. Liturgy, theology, preaching, and even the Eucharist all have their place. But sometimes God visits us in a fresh-baked loaf of bread offered in kindness.

I was tempted upon my return home to extol the virtues of this church. But I knew that would make my wife defensive, as it would anyone who is being proselytized. So I decided to play it low-key, and I suggested casually that I enjoyed the service and perhaps we could visit there as a family sometime. We did the next Sunday, and within a year found ourselves kneeling before the Bishop of Chicago to be confirmed in the Anglican communion.

ℰℐ

For me one of the most impressive features of Anglicanism was that it was at the time one of the few churches that was still a worldwide *communion*. There were some Protestant groups that had historical ties with international groups, but no real organic unity. They in no sense held each other accountable, nor did they engage in common life or mission in any regular and ongoing way. But Anglicans met regularly across borders to pray and work together and to give guidance to the international communion.

As a Presbyterian minister, I loved the different ways the church worked together nationally through its various bodies—presbytery, synod, and general assembly. But Anglicans took that to a global level. I wanted to be part of not just a regional or national church but an international church, one which took seriously the need to meet, pray, and work together from the four corners of the earth. In becoming a member of the Anglican communion, I had to give up my ordination in the Presbyterian Church. But that was not a big deal for me, because I always had believed ordination was about pastoring a local congregation. Since I was no longer a pastor of a congregation, but instead a practicing journalist, it made no sense for me to keep my ordination. At least, that's how I saw it.

As evangelicals in the Presbyterian Church in the United States of America (PCUSA), my friends and I thought of ourselves as a reform movement within the church. We were hoping to bring greater emphasis to biblical theology and evangelism, and a more evenhanded and pluralistic understanding of our political responsibilities. The PCUSA, like all mainline churches, leaned decidedly left on political issues. When I became an Episcopalian, I thought of my role as an evangelical in the same way. And if I was disturbed with some matters in the Presbyterian Church, I was deeply troubled by some things I was discovering in the Episcopal Church. In addition to what we evangelicals felt was an inadequate biblical theology, a captivity to liberal politics, and a disregard for the life of the unborn, there was theological heresy among its bishops. The most infamous, of course, was John Shelby

Spong, the Bishop of New Jersey. Among other things, he denied the deity of Jesus Christ, arguing that Jesus was adopted by God as his son, and he rejected both the virgin birth and the Resurrection of Jesus. Such views were held by a handful of bishops across the land.

So I didn't join the Episcopal Church because of the theological purity of its bishops. I'd had enough experience in a mainline denomination to know that the church is always in need of reform in one way or another. And as I said, I believed that evangelicalism was a force for reform in both the Presbyterian and Episcopal churches. Then there was this: Anglicanism was an international communion, and in the places where Anglicanism was exploding in numbers (like Africa), evangelical theology was the norm.

It took me some fifteen years to realize that the American Episcopal Church had no interest in reform of any sort, let alone the sort that evangelicals might bring to the table. Nor did it have any interest in listening to what the worldwide communion had to say about some of its decisions. This became clear during the crisis of 2003. That was the year that Gene Robinson, an openly gay priest, was elected and ordained bishop of the Diocese of New Hampshire. He was the first openly gay priest to be consecrated a bishop in a major Christian denomination that believed in the historic episcopate. Given the international nature of the Anglican communion, this became a global controversy. Without giving a blow-by-blow of what happened next, it became clear in a few months that the communion had more or less become a mere federation, split along theological lines. Even though most of the communion rejected the move by the American church, the American church rejected the counsel of the global communion.

Many people assumed the issue was human sexuality. But that was only the presenting issue. The real concerns for me and my friends were matters of theology and epistemology; that is, how do we as Anglicans together determine God's ways for us—what he wants us to believe and how he wants us to live? Naturally, evangelical Anglicans across the world believed that the Bible, as commonly read and understood throughout the history of the church, should be our lodestar. Those of a liberal persuasion had what they thought was a better idea.

This has been clearly expressed in church documents and in conversations with many Episcopalians. While some twist and turn Scripture to make it approve of same-sex relations, the intellectually honest recognize that the Bible uniformly condemns such behavior. But then they will go on to argue, "The Holy Spirit is doing a new thing." This, in fact, has become something of a mantra in Episcopal circles. In short, the Holy Spirit guided the authors of Scripture to say one thing about human sexuality in their time and place, but now the Holy Spirit is saying something different to us, who live in a different time and place. Naturally, with such an epistemology, there is no check nor consistency regarding the church's life or doctrine, other than what bishops happen to think at any given moment.

It also became clear that most bishops, the principal teachers of the church, had little appreciation of theology. As our congregation quickly divided over this issue, we were visited by one of the assistant bishops of the Chicago diocese. The church's vestry met with him in the church library. As a bishop ought, he tried to reconcile the two sides. But this is the way he went about it: He said, "It's like painting the church library. Some in the congregation want to paint it red, others want it painted blue." He went on to say that we just had to work out our differences. In short, he compared a matter of biblical and ethical gravity to an argument over decorating a room.

As our congregation began debating the matter in congregational meetings, I saw another dimension of Anglicanism that made my heart sink. As is probably clear by now, when I joined something larger than myself, I was hoping that I would be shaped by that something larger. I may have joined that something larger with some ideas of how to make it better and more healthy. But even more than that, I wanted my life and mind to be shaped by that something larger. So when I became a Presbyterian, I wanted to be shaped by a Presbyterian ethos. And when I became an Anglican, I wanted to submit myself to the traditions, theology, and liturgy of the Anglican church, in the hopes that my own heart and mind and soul would be shaped by it. In fact, I wrote a book to just this end: *Beyond Smells & Bells: The Wonder and Power of Christian Liturgy*. I crafted it mostly for newcomers to liturgical worship, especially those joining the Episcopal Church. It was not so much an attempt to explain what was happening during the liturgy as to help people see that if they participated in the liturgy, it would shape them in certain ways.

During these congregational meetings about the controversy over Scripture and human sexuality, I was surprised to discover that many Episcopalians believe no such thing. As one woman put it, "I didn't join the Episcopal Church for the church to tell me what I should believe and how I should act. I joined it because it is a place where I could discover what I wanted to believe and how I wanted to live." When she said this, the proverbial lights went on, and I realized why the church would not discipline their wayward bishops, no matter how egregious their theological errors. The church's ethos was to let people alone—to find their path, whatever it might be.

I received a hint of this a bit earlier during an interim between priests, when I served as senior warden. Leading up to an election of new vestry members, I was told that one of the candidates was living with a man outside of marriage. As a former pastor, I recognized that members of the church were "working out their salvation" and learning what that meant. One had to have patience as they grew into a greater understanding of how Christ called them to live. But it struck me as a bad idea to have such a person in a position of leadership on the vestry. It wasn't that vestry members were required to be paragons of virtue, but they were still responsible to at least try to model what the church taught and how the Bible guided us to live.

So I brought this matter up to our interim priest, and said that he might want to have a conversation with this woman and ask her to quietly withdraw her candidacy. Imagine my surprise when he said that he was not going to do that because it was none of his business how this woman wanted to lead her life. I had naïvely thought that this was very much a priest's business, the cure of souls being one of the main pillars of his calling.

30

‹›

As things came to a head during the Gene Robinson controversy, I decided I could no longer in good conscience remain a member of the Episcopal Church. One of my wife's greatest kindnesses was telling me one evening that if I wanted us to leave the church, she understood and wouldn't fight it. And this from a woman who had many strong friendships with people from both sides of the controversy. Long story short, my wife and I began attending a breakaway Anglican church, Church of the Resurrection in Wheaton. My experience in that church was extraordinary in many ways, but that will be noted in the next chapter. Let me conclude this one by noting one more aspect of Anglicanism that eventually troubled me.

For many evangelicals who make their way on the Canterbury Trail, Anglicanism is much-needed respite. As I've noted, I deeply appreciate evangelical theology, spirituality, and ethos, but there's no denying that evangelicals can become as legalistic and judgmental as the fundamentalists they think they have left behind.

Just a note here for those who might equate evangelicals with fundamentalists. From a distance, they may look the same, but inside the movements, they are very different. Evangelicals believe in "the fundamentals" (the Virgin Birth, the bodily Resurrection, the authority of Scripture, and so forth), but they are much more willing to engage all aspects of higher learning as well as life in the world. And they use that engagement to broaden their understanding of Scripture and theology, as well as shape their work in the world so they don't come across as so self-righteous. Fundamentalists have tended to be separatists, letting the world go to hell while they tried desperately to rescue a few souls. That has changed since the rise of the Religious Right, which was not only about engaging the world but changing it into its image. Still, the matter of tone is a huge difference in the two movements, one more open to engaging culture, the other more interested in fighting culture wars.

At any rate, what evangelicals discover in Anglicanism is not only a willingness to engage the world, but also the richness of liturgy and the church's appreciation of its long history and traditions. There is also a decided lack of the legalism from which many evangelicals need to escape for their own sanity. In general, Anglicans are not anxious or intense about their faith—well, except for when they first become enamored with Anglicanism. They work hard at not being judgmental, and they do not spend much time looking down their noses at others—well, except those who don't worship liturgically. Yes, to be an Anglican is to become a liturgical snob of sorts, but it is also to become a person who recognizes that you are a liturgical snob and that it is best to try to keep that in check.

All in all, Anglicanism is a comfortable faith. That's why it can be such a healing faith for people coming out of strict, authoritarian, or fundamentalist backgrounds. For such people, Anglicanism is the proverbial breath of fresh air, even if filled with incense on high holy days. But in my experience, it's the very comfortableness of this faith that is its own undoing. (At this point, I'm going to say some things that will make my Anglican friends unhappy. But what do you expect from someone who thinks he's found the true Church?) This comfortableness manifests itself in the fact that the church—in particular, the American church—has traditionally appealed to a particular niche in the culture: men and women of higher education, higher economic and social status. And that means white, upper-middle to upper class, white-collar people with a university degree or three. One would hope that across the country one would see a more varied representation of ethnicity and class. But you'd be hard-pressed to find that in Anglicanism. Both the mainline Episcopal Church and the Anglican Church in North America (ACNA) appeal to America's elite, and little else.

As Anglicanism has become more and more the "respectable" denomination, it has increasingly appealed to evangelicals who, as opposed to fundamentalists, desperately want to be accepted—not simply for their self-esteem but also because they want to win people to Jesus Christ. So it makes sense that they would want to be a part of a church that has—well, some class. You'll have a much easier time finding acceptance with friends like you if you belong to a classier church.

Christianity Today was not immune from this phenomenon. It was started explicitly to make evangelicalism more intellectually respectable among America's elite. For the last few decades, a large percentage, and at times the majority, of the editorial staff have been Anglicans. At one point, the editor in chief, managing editors for print and online, and the deputy managing editor—that is, the editorial leadership team—were all Anglicans! And because their network is packed with Anglicans, a disproportionate percentage of evangelical Anglicans have bylines in the magazine. This—combined with growing evangelical Anglican churches around Biola, Wheaton, and Gordon-Conwell, among other evangelical centers of higher learning—gives the impression that evangelicals are flocking to Anglicanism.

But all these phenomena constitute a thin slice of American evangelicalism, limited to evangelicals of certain social and economic groups. Let me say at this point that I don't find this scandalous as do some. There is nothing intrinsically wrong with a congregation or denomination identifying itself and reaching out to mostly one social/economic class, or even one ethnic or racial group. I certainly don't object to primarily Hispanic or Asian or Black churches. I can't very well criticize white churches for being white—unless of course their policies or practices deliberately exclude believers of other races.

But as an Anglican, some of the dynamics in play in this regard made me increasingly unhappy. One was this: that despite some rightful talk about concern for the poor and marginalized, and despite some generous giving to such ministries, there does not seem to be a strong and fervent witness to concern for the poor. Yes, here and there, congregations attempt to reach out to one marginalized group or another. I know of an impressive congregation in Aurora, Illinois, for example, that is trying to reach out to the predominantly Hispanic population there. But given the history and dominant ethos of Anglican religion, in either its Episcopal or evangelical incarnations, I doubt that such efforts will prove successful. More to the point: I do not believe the Anglican tradition can produce a Mother Teresa or a Dorothy Day or an Óscar Romero—that is, men and women, who number in the hundreds and thousands, who demonstrate an intense love for the poor in both word and deed. Add to that the radical witness of the monastic orders. There are a handful in Anglican circles, but the call to poverty, chastity, and obedience is simply not in the communion's DNA—at least not to the degree one finds in Catholicism.

To be fair, it's not like every Catholic parish is multiracial or multiethnic, let alone multiclass. But there is a continuing witness in the Church's life and liturgy that the Church is much more diverse than one's parish. Even though I attend a middle-class, mostly white Catholic parish, we are reminded regularly—not just in occasional sermon exhortations during Lent or on a social justice Sunday—of our duty to love the poor. Almost every day, a saint is honored who did just that. Yes, middle-class Catholics have the same temptation to substitute charitable giving for direct work with the poor, but it nearly goes without saying that the Catholic witness to working with the poor is one of its most impressive features. The longer I remained in Anglicanism and the more I flirted with Catholicism, the more this difference impressed me.

That being said, the comfortableness of the Anglican Church was clearly a much-needed blessing for me for a time. And in ways that are now obvious, it was clearly a tributary that was going to dump me into the Tiber.

CHAPTER 5

Touching the Hem of His Robe:
Mysticism

During my foray into Anglicanism, my local Anglican church, Church of the Resurrection in Wheaton, threw open a door that I had only peeked into now and then: Christian mysticism. The congregation's leaders would resist using the word "mysticism" to describe some of the gifts they bring to the table. In some evangelical circles, mysticism has nothing but negative connotations. But I use the word to talk about a range of supra-rational (not irrational) experiences where one experiences the Holy Spirit with some immediacy or is given a glimpse into eternity.

My first such experience happened on a sunny afternoon in a second-floor bedroom in Glen Ellyn, Illinois. I cannot date the experience now, but I think it happened sometime in the early 1990s. I glanced out the window, and in a vision that lasted no more than one or two seconds, I grasped intuitively and with profound assurance that the universe was one and that everything that existed was connected in some extraordinary way. I didn't understand this intellectually as I'm describing it now. It was an insight, a feeling, a perception that enabled me to grasp at some deep level that this was the way the universe is. And then it ended. It did not lead me to fall on my knees in prayer or devote myself to the religious life or start serving the poor or write a book about it. To be honest, my only reaction afterward was "That was interesting!" And since that time, I have not given it much thought. But the moment has never left me.

I've had other such moments, but none with the same sense of transcendent insight or clarity. All the others happened in moments of prayer, when the presence of God was palpable: once in a small room at Union Evangelical

Church in Mexico City, after a period of fasting; another on a beach in Cayucos, California; another still when I was nearly slain in the Spirit during a worship service at Glenbard West High School.

I do not hold much stock in the phenomenon known as slaying in the Spirit. I attended one such prayer meeting while I was serving as an associate pastor of an English-speaking church in Mexico City. We had some enthusiastic charismatics who invited me to hear an itinerant evangelist preach and then pray for people. I had taken a seat near the front, and it became obvious that the evangelist, a strong and tall male, would physically put people off-balance as he touched their forehead, and then give them a push at the end of his prayer. The susceptible collapsed in amazement. I left not a little angry.

The Church of the Resurrection (or "Rez") regularly encouraged people to receive healing prayer, but not of the dramatic sort. It was never expected that you would be healed instantly and obviously after such prayer, though you might expect the natural healing process to accelerate over the next few weeks. As far as other charismatic gifts, they were practiced quietly. If you paid close attention, you might catch the pastor praying in tongues quietly before he preached, but never was the practice encouraged from the pulpit. In private, the pastoral staff might encourage one to explore that gift, but overall the church was low key charismatic—and *never* talked about slaying in the Spirit. I had heard more than one visitor say that when they entered the sanctuary, they felt the presence of God in a powerful way, and I believed them. I never felt that myself, but who was I to deny that God met them in this way?

Rez met in the local high school auditorium at the time. During communion, worshipers were invited to approach one of the half dozen prayer ministers who stood in the side aisles. I was much taken with this practice and eventually became a prayer minister myself. There was nothing dramatic or sensational about it: You tell the prayer minister why you want prayer. The prayer minister would then ask for permission to touch you, which usually meant putting hands on your shoulder or head as he or she prayed for you. Usually, the prayer ended with the prayer minister anointing your forehead with oil and a blessing.

Nothing extraordinary was expected to happen at that moment, and nothing extraordinary was ever encouraged. After seeking healing prayer for wrenching back pain, the prayer minister reminded me that if God decided to heal me of my infirmity, it would likely be over time and in quiet ways that I would not notice.

In some respects, this was a case of undersell and overdeliver. Because, in fact, I'm convinced I was healed more than once after a visit to a prayer minister. For example, I was about to go in for knee replacement surgery and asked for quick healing. Let's just put it this way: I completely skipped using a walker (the usual routine for the first week or so) and went straight to using the cane. When my physical therapist came to my door for the first time, I walked to the door with my cane. He asked to see the patient who had just had knee surgery. I told him I was the one, and he was flabbergasted that it was me. The Lord was not on the top of his game, because I still had to do all the excruciating physical exercises for the next few weeks to completely heal. And yes, the skeptic in me suggests "coincidence" or "some patients do recover quickly." But ultimately, there is no question in my mind that the prayer minister's request for quick healing was answered.

My other requests for healing—for sciatica—were also answered. Visits to physical therapists and a chiropractor were not doing the trick as much as asking prayer ministers for a few weeks running to pray for my healing. I didn't pay much attention to my progress for some time until one day it occurred to me that my pain was gone. Completely. Again, I'm convinced of divine intervention. But notice how subtle and quiet all of this was. One could easily chalk it up to coincidence, positive thinking, and so on and so forth. I believe God hides himself even in the midst of his ordinary works, so that divine intervention could just as well be explained "scientifically." I often recall that when the disciples encountered the resurrected Jesus, some worshiped him, but "some doubted" (Matt. 28:17). God is not a flashy faith healer.

One on occasion, during worship at Church of the Resurrection, I approached a petite, thin woman of gentle spirit for prayer. Being slain in the

Spirit was the last thing on my mind, especially since Rez did not practice this bizarre ritual. I can't remember what I requested prayer for. But when she laid her delicate hand on my forehead and began praying, the world started going white, and my knees began to buckle. Sensing I was going to fall and horrified at the thought, I got a hold of myself and snapped out of it. Some would call it resisting the Spirit. Perhaps, but it would have been really embarrassing to be slain in the Spirit at that moment. Sorry, Lord.

All of these experiences were my introduction to more traditional mysticism. I'd experienced enough such moments to become intrigued with the whole idea. So I picked up a copy of Evelyn Underhill's classic, *Mysticism*. I was enthralled.

෨

Underhill opened my eyes to a way of looking at the world I had yet to take seriously. In the intellectual circles I ran in, "dualism" was a dirty word. It wasn't exactly clear why dualism was evil, but crying out "Dualism!" was sufficient to throw one's conversation partner on the defensive, or to give one justification in ignoring the rest of the argument in a book. Underhill offered a full throated defense of dualism—without ever using that word—and I was an immediate convert. Her dualism is of a basic sort: we have a body and we have a soul. Recognizing their unique characteristics is the key to comprehending human destiny.

By this time, I was well-steeped in theology, having earned an MDiv from Fuller Theological Seminary and having continued my education through much and varied reading. I had been a pastor for many years, and I knew how to talk about spiritual matters, and without fear of pride, I knew a great deal about such things. But my thinking was a muddle, or I should say more of a muddle than it is now. Certainly more of a muddle before I read Underhill. I don't know that I would have claimed to be a realist, idealist, or monist at the time, but Underhill helped me sort out my vague understandings and move in a definite intellectual and spiritual direction.

For one thing, her book confirmed my suspicions about the supernatural. In my New Testament classes at Fuller, I was assured that the miracles of Jesus, and later the early Apostles, were not to be unduly emphasized. What really attracted people to Jesus was the power of the preached word and the demonstration of active love in the church. The miraculous was almost an embarrassment to the faculty.

My first rebellion against that type of rationalism occurred with an exegesis paper I wrote on 1 Corinthians 2:1–5. In this passage Paul says that in coming to the Corinthians, he did not rely on the art of rhetoric (lofty words or wisdom) to convince them of the truth of the Gospel. Instead, he came "with a demonstration of the Spirit and of power" (1 Cor. 2:4). The common interpretation championed by my professors was that Paul eschewed the trickery of mere rhetoric and relied simply on plain language, and that God used this to show forth his power by converting those who listened. The lesson being: just speak the truth and God will use it to transform lives.

But the more I read the passage and the Acts of the Apostles, the more I became convinced that Paul, in talking about "a demonstration of the Spirit and of power," meant the miraculous—in particular, healings and speaking in tongues. Thus, even in seminary I was already flirting with a more supernatural reading of the world, which in itself is to start walking the dualist's road. Even more to the point, Underhill convinced me that not only could I enjoy a direct encounter with God, the Absolute, but that the mystics could show the way. And so I began walking down the three-fold mystical path of awakening, purification, and illumination.

All in all, the journey, despite a sublime moment or two, was a dead end.

※

Besides Underhill, I devoured *The Cloud of Unknowing*, which was more or less incomprehensible, as well as writers in the orbit of Eastern Orthodoxy. Orthodoxy is particularly amenable to the mystical tradition in many ways and is fond of referring to God in abstract and apophatic ways. Apophatic

39

spirituality attempts to grasp and approach God by negation, speaking only in terms of what may not be said about God. In contrast, cataphatic theology approaches God by affirmations, which is the usual way we speak about God: God is just, God is holy, God is omniscient, and so forth.

Apophatic theology recognizes that since God is infinite and wholly other, such descriptions ultimately misrepresent God, mainly because we're using finite words with limited meaning to comprehend the Unlimited and the One Beyond Meaning. Even to say "God exists" is to suggest he participates in something called being, which suggests that God participates in something that transcends him. This is absurd, which inclines fans of apophatic theology to say startling things like "God does not *exist*" or that "God is not a *being*." They are not championing atheism but the idea that God is so different than anything we know or can conceive of that he's beyond our categories of "existence" and "being." He has to be, of course, since he created existence and being.

This sort of spiritual exploration doesn't have to wallow in the abstract; it joins hands with the cataphatic in some ways. But in this period, I was fascinated with the apophatic. Thus my devouring, not once but three times, Belden Lane's *The Solace of Fierce Landscapes: Exploring Mountain and Desert Spirituality*. It is common to find God in the cacophony of color in a field of flowers or in a stunning ocean sunset. Lane explores how many Christian mystics, usually from the Orthodox tradition, found God when there was nothing beautiful to behold, in the loneliness of rugged mountains or the emptiness of the desert. I also read books that described contemporary practices of contemplation, like centering prayer. The idea is to empty one's mind of all thoughts through the use of a mantra, so that one might come to a place beyond words and images, a place where one is said to meet God as he is, not how he is mediated through thoughts or beauty or whatever.

While these writers said it was difficult for most people to get to that place, I found it relatively simple, moving from repeatedly praying the Trisagion "Holy God, Holy Mighty, Holy Immortal, have mercy on me" to a simple repeating of the word "holy," until my mind was filled with nothing but darkness. In the opening weeks and months of that experiment (it was an on- and off-again experiment), a few things happened to me that I am not yet able to explain. If I let myself go as I entered that darkness, I would feel something that I believed was the presence of God. I won't go into detail as to why I felt that and how that manifested itself. But I believe they were genuine encounters with the divine, and they left me with a feeling of having been cleansed and, at times, accompanied by a euphoric love for all humankind.

But here's what surprised and disappointed me: these experiences made little difference in the character and quality of my moral life. No progress as far as I could tell. One would think, after touching the hem of God's robe, as I thought I was doing, and having a rush of *agape* love run through me, which is what I felt was happening, I would begin to be transformed into someone resembling a disciple of Christ. It wasn't so. Just talk to my wife.

Such prayer sessions slowly drifted away as I became increasingly suspicious of their value. I do believe that some of them were genuine experiences of the divine. But some of them, I'm sure, were psychological self-manipulations. Some were prompted by God, some by selfish spiritual desire.

They return every so often when I practice contemplation, but I never seek them out now. Part of the reason for that is, paradoxically, the very Catholic tradition that also extols the great mystics. In the end, Platonists like Underhill end up suggesting that the body—and the physical world we inhabit—is a second-class citizen. The soul is everything in the end. But Catholic fascination with the body and the physical—God became flesh, Jesus healed physical infirmities, Jesus bodily rose from the grave, Jesus comes to us in bread and wine—suggests that the body cannot be despised or marginalized in a way many mystics seem to do. This is another tension the Catholic lives with, it seems to me: grasping that there is a spiritual reality that transcends the body, and recognizing that it is in, with, and through the body that God is known.

I also concluded that spiritual experience can become a drug, and that an addiction to this type of spirituality will lead to spiritual death. After any extraordinary spiritual experience, we will begin panting after the extraordinary spiritual experience rather than the God who gives it. We will mistake the extraordinary for God and eventually stop recognizing God in the ordinary and mundane, where he chooses to make himself known day by day. And we will eventually create a god in our image, meaning one who is known first and foremost in glory and ecstasy and spiritual success—that is, the God of spiritual and material prosperity, which is in the end a false god.

Instead, I came to believe—in part by reading of Catholic and Orthodox spiritual writers—that the God we are called to know and love is the God who meets us in the plain, boring non-events of life, at moments when he just seems like nothing more than a piece of bread handed to us by a priest—which is to say, in the moments when he seems to be nothing but absent. We meet God in his fullness in the ordinary.

CHAPTER 6

Grace-ism

It would have been convenient if these tributaries—Anglicanism and mysticism—happened in distinct stages. But they didn't. They overlapped with one another, as well as with a third tributary in which I swam to find that "something more" that evangelical faith could not supply. That third tributary was radical grace, by which I mean grace as the alpha and omega of the Christian life and understood in its most extreme sense. In other words, I was going to try to become radically Protestant—that is, to reject all moralism and works righteousness and lean completely on grace as the means and motive of my life.

Works righteousness—the idea that by our good works we earn God's favor—has traditionally been anathema to Protestants since Luther started his revolution in the 1500s. God saves us by our faith, goes the idea, not by our works. Faith is specifically faith in Jesus Christ—that is, trust that it is his life, death, and Resurrection that make the forgiveness of my sins a reality and eternal life something we look forward to with confidence. This is certainly what Catholics believe as well. It's the means of faith and grace about which Protestants and Catholics differ. But in the popular Protestant imagination, Catholicism is works righteousness and Protestantism is all about faith.

Then again, it didn't take long for Protestants to begin to traffic in one form of works righteousness or another. For example, faith in some circles has become just another work. For some, their theology leads to an unrelenting and anxious examination of the state of their soul, worrying about how much and how fervently they believe in Jesus. There is a dread of "formal religion," of just going through the motions of Christianity without having a deep and profound faith in Jesus. This has led some to regularly examine the state of their souls, to pray and, yes, *work* toward a state in which their faith is lively, genuine. I recall reading in college about the Mathers, three generations of Puritan pastors in early New England. One of them had become anxious that his faith had become dull and routine. So troubled was he that he stayed up all night demanding that God enliven his faith, as he promised he would in Scripture. It was sometime in the wee hours of the morning in which he had a palpable sense of God again.

Another temptation of works is to think that faith is more or less right belief. To believe that your works save you is mistaken belief. To believe that Jesus died for your sin and rose to give you eternal life—that is correct belief. But of course, once you begin to equate faith with right belief, it rarely stops with that simple affirmation about Jesus. It soon grows into an entire theological system that one must adhere to in order to have faith that saves. More than anything, this phenomenon has led to the dismal reality of thousands of Protestant denominations. The most extreme example of this tendency was the famous Rhode Islander Roger Williams, who kept separating himself from other Christians over matters of belief, finally refusing to have communion even with his wife because they differed over some doctrine.

Though advocates of either view of faith would deny it, it seems to me that each of these is a form of works righteousness, because they each turn the focus away from Jesus Christ and put a microscope on *our* faith, on what *I* am feeling or what *I* am believing. Some have tried to do an end-around by arguing that it is not up to us whether we have faith or not; rather, it is God who unilaterally gives us faith. That is, some are elect and some are not. How do you know if you are elect? Well, it will be evidenced in your good works. Those who do the good that God calls us to do are evidently members of the elect. Except that no one who is self-aware believes he or she is doing enough good works to justify the conclusion that they are indeed part of the elect. So this version of Protestantism leads to even more anxiety and more feverish good works in the hopes of proving—if not to others, at least to yourself—that you actually have saving faith.

I should be fair here and say that Catholics fall into these traps just as easily as do Protestants. There's plenty to works righteousness to go around. It's part of human nature to want to justify our existence and to control our destinies, or to look for a key inside ourselves to prove to ourselves that we really do have sufficient faith. All I'm saying here is that Protestants, despite their protestations to the contrary, continue to be deeply tempted by works righteousness as well.

❧

One way out of this mess is radical grace. The distinction is subtle but powerful. The emphasis moves from *me believing* in Jesus Christ to believing *in Jesus Christ*. Or more simply, the emphasis is on Jesus, period.

My believing is not what makes the difference. This is the mistake of revivalism, which has traditionally preached that Jesus may have died for the forgiveness of your sin, but you are not actually forgiven until you say the sinner's prayer and decide to have faith in Jesus. The key to salvation, then, is what I do—seek pardon and decide to follow Jesus. Jesus' death only sets up the dominoes; it is my faith that pushes them over.

To be sure, there are verses in Scripture that seem to point in that direction, like "Believe on the Lord Jesus, and you will be saved" (Acts 16:31). But a deeper theological reading of the New Testament shows that it is not belief that activates salvation; rather, it is only the means by which we recognize that we are forgiven and appropriate that forgiveness personally. "In Christ God was reconciling the world to himself, not counting their trespasses against them," says Paul in 2 Corinthians 5.

Forgiveness is a done deal, and it took place on the cross, way before we had the opportunity to believe. Jesus died not just for elect believers but for the world—the world full of decidedly sinful people, the world that put Jesus on the cross. Those are the people who are forgiven. Our faith does not make that forgiveness happen. That forgiveness happened a long, long time ago. What faith does is make that forgiveness a reality in the life of the believer. The job of evangelism, then, is not to convince people to believe or to help them have a spiritual experience so that they might be saved, but to help them understand that they are already reconciled to God. It is to tell them, in Jesus' words, "The kingdom of heaven has come near" (Matt. 3:2). Already! Or in Paul's words: "For in him all the fullness of God was pleased to dwell, and through him God was pleased to reconcile to himself all things, whether on earth or in heaven, by making peace through the blood of his cross" (Col. 1:19–20).

જ

Once you grasp this distinction, it revolutionizes the way you see the world and the way you live. As David Zahl and the Mockingbird Ministries website never tire of reminding us, our culture catechizes us into believing that, in one way or another, we must justify our lives, justify our existence. In one example, he says,

> When asked how we are doing, we used to say, "Fine" or "Well." Today, as a number of commentators have noted, the default response is "Busy." And we're not lying. Smartphones and similar devices have largely chased away the uncomfortable idleness that once characterized society, quickening the pace of life to an almost absurd degree.

> But busyness is more than a description of how we're doing; it is one of our culture's predominant indicators of worth and value, a measure of personal righteousness. The more frantic the activity, the better. The implication is that if we're not over-occupied, we are inferior to those who are. As with all law-based barometers of self-worth (beauty, wealth, influence, youth, etc.), there is no *enough*.

The Lutheran theologian Gerhard Forde questioned the traditional way of understanding sanctification, which often degenerates into a new kind of works righteousness as we try to make ourselves more holy. He sabotages that with this insight:

> Sanctification . . . is perhaps best defined as the art of getting used to the unconditional justification wrought by the grace of God for Jesus' sake. It is what happens when we are grasped by the fact that God alone justifies. It is being made holy, and as such, it is not our work. It is the work of the Spirit who is called Holy.

This emphasis on God's gracious initiative and ongoing mercy is one reason I've been attracted to the theology of Karl Barth and was happy to write a biography of Barth when asked to do so. To be clear, Barth and Lutheran theology part in many significant ways, but Barth had an absolutely clear apprehension of what author Paul Zahl calls "one-way love." (Yes, father of David—grace runs in the family apparently.) Of the literally hundreds of quotes in which Barth drives home this point, especially the first part of volume 4 of his *Church Dogmatics* (the only volume I've actually read from beginning to end!), let me choose this one:

> The divine pardon does not burst into man's willingness but his unwillingness. Man will always be a miracle and a puzzle to himself as he breaks out in this way. He will never find in himself any reason for doing so. He will not be of the opinion that he has made even the slightest contribution to it. He will rather confess freely and frankly that his own contribution is only his own great corruption, in which without any co-operation or merit of his own he is found by the divine pardon—not in his self-judgment but in the judgment of God—reached and converted to God and set on the way.

Catholic theology would want to fine-tune Barth's statement here to give more credence to our role in cooperating with the extraordinary grace given us. But Catholic theology agrees that all the glory and honor for our salvation belongs to the "pioneer and perfecter of our faith" (Heb. 12:2), Jesus Christ.

When this insight is integrated into one's life, good works emerge not as an effort to prove one's faith or to curry God's favor, but simply because one is so grateful, one is so full of love, one is finally free from playing all those self-justifying games. Instead of God's commands being an onerous duty, they can become a delight. Now you just *want to* obey the Ten Commandments, *want to* align your life with the Sermon on the Mount, *want to* love the neighbor, *want to* become as holy as Christ—not out of compulsion but real freedom.

☙

Yet here's the rub: this theology—this perception of radical forgiveness—is never completely integrated into the depths of one's soul. Most days we're just trying to get by, and God's work in Christ is just an idea and not something that alters us. In short, seeking to be holy and loving the neighbor are anything but spontaneous.

After living with the amazing reality of radical grace, you wake up one morning knowing you don't have to do anything to justify your existence, and also realizing you really don't feel like doing anything! There may still be a part of you that *wants to* do something, and yet often it's more accurate to say you *want to want to* do something. So what do you do? In my experience, here is where the teachers of radical grace are reluctant to say anything, lest it put us right back on the track of trying to justify our existence.

And this is precisely where Catholicism filled out the picture for me. It recognizes that salvation is an absolute gift, one that is not dependent on anything we do, but rather on what God has done and is doing in Jesus Christ. Many passages from the *Catechism of the Catholic Church* drive this home, but I think it appropriate in this context to quote from the 1999 *Joint Declaration on the Doctrine of Justification by the Lutheran World Federation and the Catholic Church* to point out the fundamental agreements of Lutherans and Catholics on this point:

48

In faith we together hold the conviction that justification is the work of the triune God. The Father sent his Son into the world to save sinners. The foundation and presupposition of justification is the incarnation, death, and resurrection of Christ. Justification thus means that Christ himself is our righteousness, in which we share through the Holy Spirit in accord with the will of the Father. Together we confess: By grace alone, in faith in Christ's saving work and not because of any merit on our part, we are accepted by God and receive the Holy Spirit, who renews our hearts while equipping and calling us to good works.

This is matched also in many prayers in the Catholic tradition. One of my favorites is from the diary of St. Maria Faustina:

O Great Merciful God, Infinite Goodness, today all mankind calls out from the abyss of its misery to your mercy, to your compassion. . . . We implore you, anticipate us with your grace and keep on increasing your mercy in us, that we may faithfully do your holy will all through our life and at death's hour. . . . Let the omnipotence of your mercy shield us from the darts of our salvation's enemies that we may with confidence, as your children, await your final coming.

As I've said, many days I awake not feeling all that grateful or full of love for Jesus. The joy of my salvation is not palpable. My actions for the day will not automatically emerge out of a heart feeling full of gratitude. This is when duty and obedience come into play, and why Catholic teachers insist that along with affirming the reality of unconditional mercy, there is an uncompromising call to pursue holiness. Again from the Catholic-Lutheran accord:

According to Catholic understanding, good works, made possible by grace and the working of the Holy Spirit, contribute to growth in grace, so that the righteousness that comes from God is preserved and communion with

Christ is deepened. When Catholics affirm the "meritorious" character of good works, they wish to say that, according to the biblical witness, a reward in heaven is promised to these works. Their intention is to emphasize the responsibility of persons for their actions, not to contest the character of those works as gifts, or far less to deny that justification always remains the unmerited gift of grace.

In Catholicism, as in many branches of Protestantism, there is a recognition of an awful reality: we can squander the grace that has been given us, and we can, simply put, lose our salvation. The fact that this reality sometimes fills us with fear is reason for some Protestants to reject this idea, the notion being that we should not be motivated by fear. True faith, so it goes, can only be motivated by love and gratefulness.

But again, Catholics are more realistic here. They recognize that human beings are broken, and that the Church, like its Lord, must use various human emotions to wake us up from sleepy devotion, or to call us away from the temptation to abandon the faith. In this, they are merely following the example of our Lord, who could on the one hand comfort with words like "Come to me, all you that are weary and are carrying heavy burdens, and I will give you rest" (Matt. 11:28) and at other times sternly warn, "Everyone who hears these words of mine and does not act on them will be like a foolish man who built his house on sand. The rain fell, and the floods came, and the winds blew and beat against that house, and it fell—and great was its fall!" (Matt. 7:26–27).

So, while I pray to become so enamored with the love and grace of God that good works will spontaneously arise from gratefulness, I also know that I am weak and forgetful, and I need the loving admonitions of Jesus through his Church. And while I still believe in radical grace—that salvation is the work of God from beginning to end—I also now believe in radical obedience as well, working out my salvation with fear and trembling (Phil. 2:12).

PART II
On the Tiber

CHAPTER 7

Flirting with Orthodoxy

While I was floating down one tributary and another, I was also exploring another ancient tradition that has many of the same historical and theological roots as Roman Catholicism: Orthodoxy. I became enamored with the writings of Kallistos Ware, Anthony Bloom, Thomas Hopko, Frederica Mathewes-Green, and especially Alexander Schmemann, among others. I was fascinated with the mysticism, the theology, and the transcendent mystery of its worship. When I visited an Orthodox Church, I was transported to another plane of existence.

But what initially attracted me to Orthodoxy was the no-nonsense spirituality of many of its writers. My first introduction to "the Orthodox way" I found in a small book by Mother Raphaela, *Living in Christ: Essays on the Christian Life by an Orthodox Nun*. For example, in one passage she contrasts our entertainment culture with the church's liturgy, saying, "There are many things that cannot be learned through entertainment":

> The liturgical services of the church are also in this category, most especially the Divine Liturgy. Like the education offered by a good teacher, everything that is needed is provided. Yet in order to learn, the student is forced to think to draw out the meaning, forced to develop the conclusions on his own, forced to develop his capacity for responding: for responsible and creative thinking.

So much for user-friendly worship.

I also found common-sense advice on prayer from Fr. Anthony Bloom's *Beginning to Pray*. For example, in responding to God's seeming absence during prayers, he says this:

> We complain that He does not make Himself present to us for the few
> minutes we reserve for Him, but what about the twenty-three and a half
> hours during which God may be knocking at our door and we answer, "I
> am busy, I am sorry" or when we do not answer at all because we do not
> hear the knock at the door of our heart, of our conscience, of our life.

We are embedded in a world saturated with sentimental spirituality—
evangelicalism not excluded—where church services are designed to make
one feel happy and excited about faith, and where pastoral wisdom is mostly
about comforting needy believers who find life difficult. Along come the
Orthodox to tell us to stop whining and stiffen our spines: "The Christian
life is hard. Get used to it."

As a result of all this reading, I concluded that Orthodoxy has many
strong theological and historical points regarding its claim to be the authentic church. Though Protestants, especially evangelicals, claim to be the true
heirs of New Testament Christianity, the historical record shows otherwise.
This isn't the book to detail that claim, nor do I wish to deny the truth
and goodness that Protestantism has brought and continues to bring to
worldwide Christianity. Nor can an open-minded look at Orthodoxy fail
to recognize some deep dysfunctions—for example, bitter rivalries between
the various Orthodox branches, a temptation to live in the past, and severe
legalism, among other sins. And Catholicism has had and still has serious
ethical breaches. No, my interest and attraction to these great streams was
not their ethical or ecclesial purity, but their concrete, historical connection
to the early Apostles of Jesus, and thus to Jesus himself—and the profundity
of teaching and worship that emerged from that.

One such teaching, perhaps more of an assumption, startled me as a
Protestant: the ambivalence about primitivism. Primitivism is a pillar of
Protestantism. It means simply this: what came first, what was primary, has
greater authority than what came later. Thus the Protestant assumption that

54

the earliest New Testament manuscripts are more authentic than later manuscripts. If an earlier manuscript says one thing and a later copy another, the assumption is that the later copy of that text is a mistake or an interpolation by the copyist. To put it theologically, the earlier version is viewed as closer to the God-breathed text, and thus more reliable. This is simply a given in Protestant biblical scholarship.

This is not a given in Orthodox and Catholic circles, and when I discovered this, I was floored. For example, I was startled to read in the introduction to *The Orthodox Study Bible: New Testament and Psalms* that it used the New King James Version for its modern translation of the Greek text. This surprised me because I knew that the NKJV is an update of the historic King James Version, a translation that was based on what is called the *Textus Receptus*, or the "received text." I also knew that contemporary textual critics considered it an inferior Greek text, meaning, there were earlier and therefore more linguistically authentic manuscripts upon which to ground a translation. Yet the authors of the introduction defended the authority of the *Textus Receptus* precisely because these manuscripts *came later*! The basic idea was that the Holy Spirit was still overseeing the production of Scripture, and sometimes later in the process, copyists finally got some things right.

A concrete example that presents problems for Protestants but not for the Orthodox or Catholics is John 7:53–8:11, the story of the women caught in adultery. It is one of the most moving stories in the New Testament, and accords perfectly with Jesus' treatment of the self-righteous and sinners we find elsewhere in the Gospels. But this passage is not found in any of the earliest manuscripts we have of the Gospel of John. So, many modern translations put the passage in brackets and note this fact. In this, they show their unwillingness to follow their own principles, which would be to leave out the passage and, at best, put it in a footnote.

But what if the earliest is not always the most authentic? What if early writers forgot to include a story or a detail? Or what if local ecclesial pressures discouraged the writer from including something? And what if this story or these details remained alive in the oral tradition? And what if fifty or a hundred or two hundred years later, a copyist came along and said, "Enough is enough. This bit belongs!" Or what if the Holy Spirit enabled a copyist to discover a long-forgotten early manuscript with the crucial story in it, and so he decided to insert it in his copy? And so on.

Of course, this is conjecture, but it suggests that earliest is not necessarily most authentic. And with that, one key pillar of my Protestantism suffered a serious crack. It made me question many Protestant criticisms of Orthodox and Catholic beliefs and practices, like "It isn't in the Bible; it isn't in the early church even; it didn't become prominent until a later century; therefore, it is not something sanctioned or inspired by the Holy Spirit." Unless, of course, the Holy Spirit continued to be alive and well after the New Testament authors died; unless the Holy Spirit continued to lead the Church into "all the truth," as Jesus promised in John 16:13.

In short, I started to become convinced that any given tradition, even one that came substantially later, could be just as God-breathed as some passage in the New Testament that we might know came from the lips of Jesus himself. The Orthodox balk at anything new that comes after the first five ecumenical councils, their assumption being that divine inspiration ceased at that point. I'm not inclined to buy that assumption for reasons too complex to go into here. Suffice it to say, this crack in the pillar of primitivism pushed me to eventually believe that the Holy Spirit is still seeking to bring the Church into all truth, and that he does it precisely *through* the Church, over time, as scholars and bishops wrestle with matters and as the laity live them out.

At any rate, my exploration of things didn't demand an instant conversion to Orthodoxy or Catholicism. Evangelical religion may be inadequate in many respects, but it is still a work of God for the good of his faithful and for his world. Still, I seriously explored becoming Orthodox, partly because, hoping against hope, I thought I might be able to continue at *Christianity Today*. I believed I could convince the president and the board that since Orthodoxy didn't have a pope and magisterium like Catholicism, readers wouldn't find it as objectionable. I could have my true church *and* work in a ministry like *Christianity Today*.

So I began attending a local Orthodox parish, and had many a conversation with members and the parish priest. I recall with special fondness the hospitality of Frederica Mathewes-Green when I visited her to talk about my journey. In fact, I decided to give Orthodoxy a test run. One Lent I participated as best as I could in the Orthodox Lenten fast, which is rigorous by Catholic and Protestant standards. It more or less amounts to going on a vegan diet. That was a challenge, but not nearly the challenge that Easter was.

The Orthodox liturgical calendar is not synced with the Protestant and Catholic calendars, and this particular year, the Orthodox were still in the middle of Lent when the rest of Christendom was celebrating Easter. The rest of Christendom included my family. So when my wife and I visited my son and his family on Easter, they prepared a lavish feast that was anything but vegan. Awkward to say the least. It occurred to me that, if I became Orthodox, this would be the case for the rest of my life—having to recuse myself from celebrating with my family while they rejoiced in the Resurrection.

That's when it became clear that Orthodoxy in many respects is a family religion. It's nigh impossible to be an Orthodox Christian without the support of immediate and often extended family. Given the importance of food in that tradition and the many guidelines surrounding it, eating is very much a communal event. If I was going to convert to Orthodoxy, I saw that I'd have to encourage my wife and my grown children to convert as well—and, aside from a miracle, I could not see them converting. My journey into Orthodoxy came to a screeching halt that Easter season.

It may seem like awkwardness over Easter dinner is a superficial reason to reject a historic church, and perhaps it is. But I don't think Orthodoxy or Catholicism would agree. Food is woven into the history of salvation, beginning with the taste of forbidden fruit and culminating for the present in a Sacred Meal. Both communions ground their teaching and ethics in a profound appreciation of the physical realities of life, which certainly include family. And while there are occasions when one must choose between faith and family, most of the time we're called to figure out how to make those work together, even if you and your family don't share the same faith.

Leaving Orthodoxy was not therefore a rejection of Orthodoxy. In fact, when one moves from Orthodoxy to Catholicism, one is not actually leaving Orthodoxy because of the intimate and historical ties between the two communions. As the *Catechism* puts it, quoting older church documents:

> The Eastern churches that are not in full communion with the Catholic Church celebrate the Eucharist with great love. "These Churches, although separated from us, yet possess true sacraments, above all—by apostolic succession—the priesthood and the Eucharist, whereby they are still joined to us in closest intimacy." A certain communion *in sacris*, and so in the Eucharist, "given suitable circumstances and the approval of Church authority, is not merely possible but is encouraged." (CCC 1399)

So, since Orthodoxy was not going to work at a practical level, that left Catholicism as the only option if I was going to become a part of the historic Church. Yet if family was the obstacle to Orthodoxy, employment was the stumbling block to becoming Catholic.

CHAPTER 8

Disembarking at Rome

After Catholicism was put on the fast track, it wasn't long before one event more or less sealed the deal intellectually.

As I worked out at the gym and drove around town, I listened to an audio version of Bishop Robert Barron's *Catholicism*, a reasoned and lyrical apologetic for the Catholic faith. He walks readers through the intellectual shoals of modern philosophy, sometimes to show its failures, sometimes to recognize its keen insights, but always to show how Catholicism embraces the best of human philosophy and takes it deeper. At the same time, he helps readers marvel at the beauty of Catholicism. While showing the intellectual coherence of its more controversial doctrines, like the Immaculate Conception, he also extols its poetry (Dante!) and architecture (Notre Dame!) and lived life (Francis of Assisi and Mother Teresa!).

By the time I finished reading it for the first time, I had become rationally convinced that Rome was home for me. I was in the Tiber and had docked at Vatican City. My friend Adam was also converting at the time, and we determined to watch the video version with our wives to help them see where we were coming from. (Okay—with the hope of converting them.) The plan to view the videos never took place, for which I'm sure our wives are grateful. Who wants to spend many an evening with dreamy-eyed converts?

But as I suggested at the end of the last chapter, for the next few months I was in limbo, mentally a Catholic and still editor in chief of *Christianity Today*.

❧

It wasn't long after reading *Catholicism* that I started attending the Sunday evening service at a local Catholic church, far enough away from Wheaton where I wouldn't be recognized: Sts. Peter and Paul in Naperville. And after doing that for a month or so, I also decided once more to listen to Barron's book. It was a one-two punch that won the final round.

As I listened to Barron's book again, I was even more impressed with his erudition and his grasp of the multidimensional wonder of the Catholic Church. Chapter by chapter, he explored its various nooks and crannies, highlighting some key figure or key event or artistic endeavor in Catholic history. It was the end of the book that overwhelmed me. In a coda, he clarifies that, for all its varied gifts, his book was not about the Catholic Church but about God, a God who makes himself known—and "how God uses Catholicism to utter his Word." For reasons that will soon be clear, I have to quote that passage extensively.

For I am certain that God speaks through the sinuous arguments of Aquinas, through the upward-thrusting lines of the Cologne Cathedral, through the artfully crafted story of tortured Job, through the tear-stained pages of Augustine's *Confessions*, through the letters that Paul wrote from prison, through the profession of faith given by Simon Bar-jona at Caesarea-Philippi, through a speech offered to puzzled philosophers on the Areopagus in Athens, and through the missionary journeys of Matteo Ricci and Francis Xavier. I am sure that God whispers in the apse mosaic in San Clemente, in that Noah's ark that is Notre Dame Cathedral, in the statues of the apostles in the Basilica of St. John Lateran, in the infallible umpiring of the popes, in the Rhapsodic Theatre of young Karol Wojtyla, and in the rhythmic "we want God" chant of the Warsaw throng.

And I am convinced that God communicates himself in the angel's "Ave" to a Galilean girl, in the torch-lit parade in Ephesus in honor of Theotokos, in the heavenly lady who appeared to an Indian man on his way to Mass, in what appears to the world to be the utter uselessness of the sacred Liturgy, in transfigured signs of bread and wine, in the troubled hearts of two women who left the presence of Pope Leo XIII in tears, in the Birkenau gas chamber in which a brave and brilliant nun died, and in a call heard on the way to Darjeeling: "help the poorest of the poor." I am persuaded that God expresses himself in the electric intensity of the Sainte-Chapelle, in the dingy coffee shop on 111th Street that became, for a young spiritual seeker fresh from Mass, the Elysian fields, in the mystical poetry of a Spanish friar madly in love, in the pierced heart of Teresa of Avila, in the epiphany at the corner of Fourth and Walnut, in the severity of Lough Derg, in the chants and dances that honor the young martyrs of Uganda, and in the singing of the fiery Seraphim, burnt by their proximity to the holy.

I was listening to this as I was driving, and I started weeping so hard I had to pull to the side of the road. It would not be good if, during a mystical moment, I ran over a pedestrian. And it was mystical: when he finished the coda, having just beautifully expressed the very catholicity of this Church, I knew I had become a Catholic in my heart.

☙

Next came the will. As was my new habit, I continued attending Mass at Sts. Peter and Paul, but I never partook in Communion. I understood the Catholic theology of the Eucharist: that it is a sign of real, sacramental, and institutional unity, and not merely a sentiment about the "spiritual" unity of Christians. One should not receive the Eucharist until one declares one's allegiance to the Roman Catholic Church. There was also another matter—that is, one fully joins this Church when one is confirmed. And since I had not yet been confirmed, there was to be no Eucharist.

But during one Mass, as congregants lined up to go forward, I had an insight that startled me with its simplicity, if not liturgical correctness. I recalled that I had been baptized as a Catholic and as a boy *had taken First Communion*! I was essentially living between the time of First Communion and Confirmation, when Catholics are permitted to take Communion. Granted, mine was a particularly long gap between the two sacraments, but for some of us, catechetical teaching takes a few decades to sink in. At any rate, since my desire was now clearly to become confirmed as soon as possible, I joined the line and partook of the Eucharist.

I knew that the order of things was not quite right. Given my long trek in Protestantism, I should have first talked to a priest in order to receive permission to receive the Eucharist. I also realized, for various reasons—travel time for one—that Sts. Peter and Paul would not become my home parish. So I made an appointment with Father Dan at St. Michael's in Wheaton. I told him what had been happening to me and requested permission to take Communion. He said he didn't see a problem, especially since I had in fact received First Communion when I was a boy. He only asked that I prepare my confession and partake in the sacrament of Reconciliation. I was only too happy to do so. It was a tearful confession of a deeply contrite heart. I started attending weekday Mass at St. Michael's as often as I could, as well as Sunday Mass.

❧

All of this took place in the late summer and early fall of 2018, when I was still editor in chief of *Christianity Today*. Technically and truly, I was still not fully a Catholic—that doesn't happen until the sacrament of Confirmation. I had that distinct sense that it was still not time to leave CT, but I felt I could carry out my duties in good faith. Again, my job wasn't to convert readers to Catholicism, but to help them be more faithful evangelicals, a mission I had no trouble affirming. I also looked at the calendar and knew I would probably leave the ministry in 2020 at the latest, when I would retire. I accepted the fact that I would have to live a dual existence for a couple of years.

As 2019 unfolded, and as I increasingly recognized that I was heading toward retirement, I had settled on writing a book that would pull together my greatest concerns about and hopes for the evangelical movement I had been embedded in for over half a century. It began with a series of essays online called "The Elusive Presence," but then became a book that was published in 2020: *When Did We Start Forgetting God?: The Root of the Evangelical Crisis and Hope for the Future.*

As I finished preparing the online essays for publication, I had a distinct feeling that my time at CT was over, that I had done what needed doing. I could see that after this book, I would not have anything more to contribute to the movement, as least when it came to spiritual theology, my greatest passion in all my years of service.

During this period, I told key members of the executive team, especially our president, Harold Smith, that I was planning on being confirmed in the Catholic Church when I retired—just to be as up-front as possible. They were surprised, but didn't think I needed to immediately quit my post. And when a new president, Timothy Dalrymple, was hired in May of 2019, he had already been briefed. He didn't see it as a problem since I would be retiring in a little over a year, and especially since I had no interest in using CT as a vehicle for Catholic evangelism. Still, I also told him that if he had someone in mind for editor in chief, I'd be happy to retire earlier and step aside. By the end of that summer, he had decided to do just that, and plans were set in place for Daniel Harrell to step into my shoes after I retired on January 3, 2020.

As events in late December of 2019 show, apparently there was one more thing I had to contribute at CT, whether I liked it or not. CT rarely weighs in on things political. But because CT had addressed both Richard Nixon's and Bill Clinton's impeachment hearings, I felt CT should say something about President Trump's. So I laid out, in the strongest terms, what I thought the issues were for the evangelical movement. I wasn't trying to fashion a blistering statement on my way out the door (as some have suggested), but only to compose a bracing call to those fellow evangelicals whose devotion to President Trump bordered on idolatry. I knew of course that it would be controversial within our movement, but I felt that the controversy would be a family matter.

Within ten minutes of publication, I received a call from Sarah Pulliam Bailey at *The Washington Post*, and then a few minutes later an email from Emma Green at *The Atlantic*, followed by invitations to appear on NPR and CNN the next morning. Ah, this was of interest to more than evangelicals. The next few weeks were crazy with interviews, podcasts, emails, phone calls, and so forth—in short, without me manipulating media whatsoever, or even wishing for such a reaction, it became a significant event in the life of evangelicalism and the nation. I mention this only to suggest that it's made me wonder if perhaps *this* was the reason the Lord had me stay at CT.

All I can say is that the response to the editorial was a confirmation that it was indeed time to leave CT, and I was grateful that my retirement was a couple of weeks away. While the editorial overall gained subscriptions and a great deal of positive press, it also generated a fair amount of criticism, especially from some major donors to CT. This created problems for the president and the board that would have made my continuing at CT difficult if not impossible. As it turned out, even my emeritus connections—the posting of my ongoing weekly newsletter, *The Galli Report*, on CT's website—had to be severed. (I moved the newsletter to my own site.) While such developments saddened me—I had, after all, given my best thirty years to the ministry—I understood these political realities and the need for CT to distance itself from me.

At any rate, with my retirement in January 2020, I was able to set a date to become confirmed. The first date (April 2020) was canceled, because it fell right in the middle of the coronavirus lockdown. The second date (September) had to be a small affair, in which only the confirmand's sponsor was allowed to attend. I was hoping to invite lots of my friends and have a reception at my home afterward, but COVID-19 canceled that idea. So in some ways, Confirmation was anticlimactic. Nothing mystical happened during the service, though I did find myself in tears now and then. Not even my wife, who remains Anglican, could attend the service, but she prepared a wonderful reception for a few close friends afterward. But I did have a distinct feeling all day that I had arrived home, and the home was the size of St. Peter's Basilica.

❧

So, when did I "become" a Catholic? In one sense, it happened at my infant Baptism, in another at my Confirmation. But how it all worked itself out in my adult life—well, it was a long journey, as I followed many tributaries along the way, with each stage feeding into the next.

There is this reality of course: one never can fully become a Catholic in this life. Catholicism is too deep and wide and tall for anyone to be able to completely embrace it, let alone comprehend it. It would be like trying to count the grains of sand on a stretch of a California beach, or straining to wrap your arms around a giant redwood.

Indeed, to become a Catholic is to be grafted onto a great tree whose trunk reaches the heavens and whose branches extend across the world, giving shade to millions upon millions living in the nooks and crannies of every nation and culture. It is a gigantic tree, yes, and yet it keeps growing, year after year, century after century, and each of us who have been grafted on grow with it. One can even say the Catholic Church itself is still becoming Catholic, until that great and glorious day when it meets its Lord face-to-face.

PART III
The True Church

CHAPTER 9

The Church in Its Fullness

In this part of the book, I look at themes that were swirling in my head and heart over long stretches of time. They don't fit neatly into a chronological narrative, as I have attempted up to this point. And yet they played key roles in the conversion of my heart, mind, and soul. I've recently realized that these themes find their center in the Church—that is, the one, holy, catholic, and apostolic Church we confess in the Creed. To put it another way, this section might be loosely construed as a defense of the Catholic Church being "the true Church." In using that phrase, I'm not suggesting that other churches are false. I could hardly say that given my lasting and deep appreciation for how evangelicalism nurtured me for so many decades. What I mean can be explained by a simple analogy.

Among my many interests has been woodworking. Sometimes that has meant fine woodworking, as in making furniture. Mostly it has been general carpentry. One essential tool in this enterprise is a table saw. For carpentry, a portable table saw is perfectly adequate. Large parts of it are made of heavy plastic or light metals like aluminum, so that it can be carried to and from a job site. With it you can cut a piece down to the sixteenth of an inch in accuracy. It's always not exact-exact, but for general carpentry—framing, flooring, and the like—it does the job splendidly.

But when I built furniture—well, that's a different story. For that I once bought a massive, heavy (not portable in the least) industrial table saw, with a high-end fence to guide the wood. It was somewhere in the neighborhood of five or six hundred pounds. It also had a number of dials and mechanisms to bring the blade and fence and table top into precise alignment. It was especially meant to be used with hard and expensive woods like oak or mahogany.

It was designed to cut precisely. For example, when cutting strips to create an oak table, the strips had to fit together with no gaps between them, perfectly straight, perfectly true, not off by even 1/64 of an inch, or it would show.

The portable table saw is, one might say, true enough and perfectly adequate for carpentry. But if you're doing fine woodworking and need precision, the industrial table saw is the way to go. If you cut a piece of oak 3 1/16 inches wide with the portable table saw, it will be awfully close to 3 1/16 inches wide, give or take 1/32 of an inch. If you cut it with the industrial saw, it will be 3 1/16 inches. Exactly. The industrial saw cut is not "true enough." It's just *true*.

Naturally, the analogy isn't perfect; theologically, the nature of the true Church is much richer and more complex. For example, one could say from a Catholic perspective that the so-called Protestant "churches" are better understood as parachurch ministries. Yet high-level theology is not my interest here. In terms of day-to-day spiritual matters, the analogy works as far as it goes. Protestant churches are the portable saws of the faith, adequate in many ways. A Baptism in a Protestant church is in fact a genuine Baptism. When someone trusts in Christ at an evangelical revival, it's a genuine expression of saving faith. When a Bible teacher exposits the Word of God, lives are genuinely changed by the Holy Spirit.

That being said, I find it difficult to conclude that Protestantism represents the one, holy, catholic, and apostolic Church, except in an abstract and idealistic way. And if there is anything that Catholicism has taught me, it's to distrust the abstract, and to notice how the faith is lived—not as an idea in the mind but with one's feet firmly planted on the ground.

I don't mean to suggest that the Catholic Church is the perfect church, that it lives impeccably as the one, holy, catholic, and apostolic Church day in and day out. The Catholic Church, too, has sins to confess and shortcomings to acknowledge—more of that in a bit. But in my reading and experience, I believe it lives out its oneness, its holiness, its catholicity, and its apostolicity more authentically and fully than does any Protestant expression of the faith. Naturally, this is an assertion that would take a book to defend, so here I acknowledge that I'm only asserting what I've concluded and giving a few examples that led me to this conclusion.

Of course, there is a theological and mystical sense in which the Catholic Church is already perfectly one, holy, catholic, and apostolic by virtue of its founding and calling in Christ. Again, that is not my interest here. It's how that mystical perfection is worked out in the daily life of the Church. One might say that, even when it is not perfectly true to its calling, it is nonetheless true, if for no other reason than it has the theological and ecclesial dials and mechanisms to recalibrate itself in every generation.

This is a clumsy way of affirming St. John Henry Newman's insight about the development of doctrine. The early debates about the relationship of Father, Son, and Holy Spirit did not come into focus until the fourth century, just as the relationship of the Eucharistic bread and Christ's body wasn't clear until the Fourth Lateran Council in 1215. And if there is a development of doctrine, in which a more complete understanding of revelation is enjoyed, so there is a development of practice. Who in 1900 would have imagined lay people offering the Host to parishioners during the Liturgy of the Eucharist, or in the medieval era of imperious popes that someday, the papacy would be consistently characterized by the humility of men like, most recently, Pope Francis?

To recalibrate, though, is not to question its trueness. It is to suggest that it is an institution, built on the sure foundation of the Apostles and prophets and the gracious words of Jesus, that has everything it needs to be the true Church in practice. It seems to me this is much more than can be said about our Protestant brothers and sisters. This may seem harsh, but as a Protestant friend once said to me when I apologized for such brashness, "You wouldn't be Catholic if you didn't think the Catholic Church was the true Church." There is that.

This, then, is the theme of part III: why I've come to believe that the Roman Catholic Church is the true Church. I'm not trying to convince anyone else of this assertion, as I'm wise enough to know holes can blow open my reasons. In fact, I've long believed that every belief has holes and weaknesses, and that the best one can do in this life is to agree that these particular holes and weaknesses are less a problem than if one were to hold an alternate view. That being said, this book is about my journey, and thus it is about my understanding of matters Catholic, however flawed and inadequate.

We begin then with the Church being one.

CHAPTER 10

One

I cannot recall when the unity of Jesus' Church first gripped my imagination. Though I was a part of both Presbyterian and Anglican bodies, for whom ecumenical efforts were *de rigueur*, such conversations never held my interest. It seemed that when it came to other Protestants, we were more or less on the same page theologically, and any differences that divided us could be lived with. In fact, we were living with them daily as we cooperated in all sorts of efforts, from civil rights marches to figuring out how to help the homeless in our communities.

The point of contention usually boiled down to church structure and how decisions were made. Baptists insist on a polity resembling pure democracy, Presbyterians favor representative democracy, and Methodists and Anglicans love their bishops. We each recognized each other's Baptisms and welcomed each other to the Lord's supper. But if you didn't govern a church the way I like it, we couldn't join together in any organic, institutional way.

I believe that one reason for this reluctance is that, as much as Protestants jealously guard their institutional practices, I'm not sure they really believe in institutions—that is, the bodily nature of our current reality. Perhaps for practical reasons, yes—for organizing large relief efforts, for ensuring the quality of ministerial credentials, for holding one another accountable at some level, and so on. But when push comes to shove, and one doesn't want to abide by a denomination's polity, one can just hop over to another denomination. And no one cares that you do, really. No harm, no foul. From a Protestant point of view, one church is more or less as good as the next. The church is not to be equated with this or that institution but instead is considered a *spiritual fellowship* of all Christians everywhere. In other words, the church is everywhere—and therefore nowhere. That at least is how I came to see things over time.

This is one reason I believe Protestant denominations number in the thousands. Organic, institutional, unified Christianity just doesn't matter. In this respect, I suspect my Protestant brothers and sisters of a kind of Gnosticism, wherein the bodily reality is marginalized in the interests of spiritual reality. Another reason: somewhere along the way, Protestants decided that heresy was a worse sin than schism. That is, for Protestants, it has been crucial that we who gather under the umbrella of a church or denomination agree on the fundamentals of the faith, which include matters of church polity. And if we can't, then we are free to leave said church and wander off to start another. To break away from the current, concrete body of Christ to which I belong—to create a schism between believers—is not nearly as troubling as failing to hold right beliefs.

As I said, since doctrinal differences don't seem to divide Protestants as much as they used to, theology is not a leading cause of new divisions today—although the various breaks due to differences on biblical authority surrounding the issue of human sexuality might be the exception that proves the rule. And frankly, not even church structure is in play sometimes. Instead, most church splits are driven by one group finding a decision of the pastor or church board untenable—from ignoring financial problems in the church, to deciding whether to expand facilities, to (and this is perhaps the most contentious) determining what type of music and instruments will be used in worship. These are often couched in theological language, but at heart the division is over personality or policy. Given that Protestant denominations number in the thousands, it would be fair to conclude that schism seems to be built into Protestant DNA.

℘

No Protestant imagines that in breaking away from a church or denomination, they are ignoring something that was crucial for their Lord, as expressed in

Jesus' high priestly prayer in John 17.

> As you, Father, are in me and I am in you, may they [the disciples] also be
> in us, so that the world may believe that you have sent me. The glory that
> you have given me I have given them, *so that they may be one*, as we are one,
> I in them and you in me, *that they may become completely one*, so that the
> world may know that you have sent me and have loved them even as you
> have loved me. (John 17:21–23; emphasis added)

Given that his death is but a few hours away, this might be considered Jesus'
"last will and testament" for his disciples. It is clear that, more than anything
else, Jesus wants his followers to be one. To put it another way: he appears
not all that concerned to preserve them from heresy but very concerned to
preserve them from schism. This is not to suggest that doctrine is superfluous,
as the chapter on the Church's apostolicity will show. But it does suggest that
pride of place belongs to unity. This is likely the reason that, when the creeds
outline the key marks of the Church, they begin with "one."

In my experience, Catholics don't have Jesus' high priestly prayer at the
front of their minds day to day, but the unity that pervades that prayer is
now built into their DNA. Catholics are reluctant to divorce themselves from
the Church. Having disagreements in the Church, some over crucial issues,
is just part of being a Catholic. You just don't up and leave when you find
something disagreeable. You may go to another parish; you may stop going
to Mass; you may sit and fume at what you perceive to be the Church's
obstinacy. But you still consider yourself a Catholic.

In the Catholic way of seeing the world, the Church is not an ideal,
not primarily a spiritual fellowship as it is in the Protestant mind. For the
Catholic, the Church is a concrete institution in which Christ takes on
flesh and lives among us, "full of grace and truth." I repeat the words of the
Incarnation as expressed in John's Gospel (John 1:14) precisely because, in
Catholicism, the Church is the continuation of the miracle of Incarnation. It
not only administers seven sacraments that concretely communicate Christ

to us; it is itself a sacrament of Jesus. From the *Catechism*:

> "The Church, in Christ, is like a sacrament—a sign and instrument, that
> is, of communion with God and of unity among all men." The Church's
> first purpose is to be the sacrament of the inner union of men with God.
> (CCC 775)

St. Augustine makes the connection stronger:

> Let us rejoice then and give thanks that we have become not only Chris-
> tians, but Christ himself. Do you understand and grasp, brethren, God's
> grace toward us? Marvel and rejoice: we have become Christ. For if he is
> the head, we are the members; he and we together are the whole man. . . .
> The fullness of Christ then is the head and the members. But what does
> "head and members" mean? Christ and the Church.

I am most fond of Joan of Arc's summary: "About Jesus Christ and the
Church, I simply know they're just one thing, and we shouldn't complicate
the matter." Few Catholics would be able to express this reality in words, but
they feel it in their souls: to leave the Catholic Church is in some sense to
leave God. Thus their hesitancy to abandon Mother Church.

To be sure, some Catholics leave the Church, some out of disgust over
some doctrine or malfeasance, and some because they have experienced spiritual renewal in an evangelical church. While many of these converts eventually make their way back to the Church, others simply adopt the Protestant
mentality of church-hopping as they search for a fellowship that better meets
their needs. As such, these folks have left the Catholic Church both formally
and intuitively—meaning they have abandoned the Catholic sensibility that
the Church is one. And yes, while some Catholics leave the Roman Church
to start a Catholic church that is purer in their view—a decidedly Protestant
motive—the number of Catholic breakoffs only number in the dozens, not in

the thousands. This suggests that even Catholic schismatics remain imbued with the sensibility that drives Jesus' prayer.

℘

There are only two Christian bodies that have remained institutionally one since the beginning: the Roman Catholic Church and the Orthodox Church. To be sure, these two communions alienated one another a thousand years after Christ's Resurrection, but both have striven to remain unified in themselves and connected to the Church of the earliest Apostles. Today, leaders in both communions regret and repent of their split, and are seeking ways to reconnect in concrete, institutional ways.

Five hundred years after that momentous split, a significant portion of Christians were separated from the Roman Catholic Church—some by choice, some by excommunication. As Catholic historians acknowledge today, the Church did indeed need reform in many ways, and Protestants were often justified in their anger and dismay at the Church. But today, five hundred years later still, we are in a different situation. The Roman Church has reformed (fine-tuned the table saw!), and it has clarified many of its doctrines that, in the 1500s, confused many believers about the nature of saving faith. In sum, many crucial things that divided Protestants and Catholics are no longer in play.

Take the doctrine of justification by faith, perhaps the greatest dispute back in the day. Typical in Protestant polemics is the notion that Catholics are said to believe in works righteousness—that one earns God's forgiveness by one's merit. But as the *Catechism* explains it:

> Justification has been *merited for us by the Passion of Christ* who offered himself on the cross as a living victim, holy and pleasing to God, and whose blood has become the instrument of atonement for the sins of all men. (CCC 1992)

Our justification comes from the grace of God. Grace is *favor*, the *free and undeserved help* that God gives us to respond to his call to become children of God, adoptive sons, partakers of the divine nature and of eternal life. (CCC 1996)

One crucial difference to one group of Protestants might be this:

Justification establishes *cooperation between God's grace and man's freedom*. On man's part it is expressed by the assent of faith to the Word of God, which invites him to conversion, and in the cooperation of charity with the prompting of the Holy Spirit who precedes and preserves his assent: "When God touches man's heart through the illumination of the Holy Spirit, man himself is not inactive while receiving that inspiration, since he could reject it; and yet, without God's grace, he cannot by his own free will move himself toward justice in God's sight." (CCC 1993)

The Reformed and Lutherans, in general, subscribe to monergism, the belief that justification is fully and only the work of God and that we play no role in it whatsoever. We're completely passive; God is the only one who is active. But two things to note.

First, I'm not convinced even monergists really believe this. Because when they evangelize the lost, they entreat them to put their trust in Jesus. Logically, they should end their evangelistic pleadings with "I hope God will do that for you." But no, they usually call for some step of faith, some human effort. It has always struck me as disingenuous—after pleading with a person to come to faith, and after they do so—to assert that this, according to the monergists, is simply a sign that God overwhelmed that person's will from start to finish.

There is one thing that monergists have going for them: it sure *feels* as if God has done everything. The analogy I find helpful is this: the ship on which I've been traveling has sunk, and I'm stranded in the middle of the ocean. Along comes a rescue ship, from which someone throws me a life preserver. I clutch on to it for dear life and am pulled to safety on the rescue ship. My first reaction is not to pat myself on the back for grabbing the life preserver, for cooperating with the person who threw the life preserver. To be sure, if I hadn't grabbed it, I wouldn't have been saved. But my entire focus, mind and heart, is on those who rescued me. Synergists—most Protestants and all Catholics—say, yes, we have to grab the life preserver. But their unrelenting focus is on the grace and work of God in salvation. So when it comes to justification, the majority of Protestants agree with Catholics on the need for people to respond to God's "prevenient grace." And despite having to clutch the life preserver, we give God all honor and praise for his grace.

That's one example. I could now pull out any number of teachings from Vatican II and the *Catechism* that convinced me that a continued separation from the Church was pretty hard to defend on purely theological grounds. My Protestant sensibilities objected here and there during the last few years before my conversion, but those objections paled in comparison to Jesus' will for the Church to be one. When I came to this conclusion, the options boiled down to two for me: work as a Protestant for reunification with Catholics, or join the Roman Catholic Church. It seems to me we need good men and women who are working both the angles.

For a reunification to take place, somebody has to give up something, and that something is often perceived as essential. Thus the fact that progress of Protestant-Catholic unity grinds to a halt at some point. But now that the Roman Church has acknowledged its corruption and the theological confusion it sometimes engendered in the late Middle Ages, and also has a rightful claim to being the original Church that remains institutionally and concretely connected to the earliest Apostles—well, as a Protestant, I had a moral obligation to rejoin Mother Church, even if I were to find myself still balking at some of its doctrines and practices. Why? For no greater reason than Jesus' high priestly prayer: *that we be one as he is one with the Father.*

Similar to my experiences in the Presbyterian and Anglican worlds, there are some things in Catholicism that don't fit easily or naturally in my heart and mind. After all, I cannot immediately shake off half a century of evangelical ethos and bias. Early on, I was concerned about possible idolatry, especially regarding Mary and the saints. But a reading of the liturgy and the *Catechism* quickly clarifies that Catholics only worship God, though they give honor to Mary and the saints, just as we give honor to loved ones who have gone before us. But don't Catholics pray to Mary and the saints? Only in the same way that we ask others who are bodily with us to pray for us; we are essentially praying for them to pray for us.

The Immaculate Conception and bodily Assumption of Mary also made me wonder; neither seem to be substantially grounded in Scripture. Also, transubstantiation seemed unreal to me. Without going into great detail, in the end, my concerns were grounded in a deep suspicion of the Church's authority, especially papal authority—and a refusal to humbly submit to the greater, time-tested wisdom of a communion that has been thinking about these things for over two millennia. It strikes me as a sign of hubris that I would bring my lonely conscience and limited understanding and pit it against the depth and the breadth of the Church's teaching across the ages.

As I've suggested, this doesn't mean Catholics don't wrestle with doctrine and practice. It doesn't mean one can never ask questions. It doesn't mean you throw your mind away. But what it does mean is that, rather than simply "protesting" or rebelling, you enter into such matters with the attitude of someone who is seeking the truth with deep respect for the tradition and authority of the Church.

But one has to admit that there remain some crucial issues of great gravity that make some Protestants refuse to even approach the Tiber. Like: Catholics don't sing hymns robustly! And they love their raffles! And look at their sentimental religious art! And too many candles! Kidding aside, it is fair to say that to enter Catholicism is to enter a different religious culture, and yes, this is alienating at times. But I never understood that discomfort as a serious impediment.

So, yes, there are things to give up, things that require humility and patience, things to get used to when becoming a Catholic. It's not unlike getting married. As my wife and I will testify, you can't be married for nearly half a century and not have had some pretty difficult moments. But such is the journey on the way to becoming one, even as Jesus and the Father are one.

CHAPTER 11

Holy

As I've suggested, the claim that the Church is holy is first and foremost a statement about its ontological reality: it is the body of Jesus Christ, the Holy One, and thus, by definition, holy. But here I want to talk about the on-the-ground reality of the Church's holiness.

To claim today that the Catholic Church is holy on the ground seems absurd. For many people, the Catholic Church is known for priests and bishops abusing boys and young men, all under the protection of the hierarchy. Sexual assault and authoritarianism all rolled into one. This in turn brings to mind many of the Church's heinous sins, from the merciless killing of Muslims during the Crusades, to the vicious persecution of Jews during the Inquisition, to the hedonistic lifestyles of some medieval popes. The Church may have a long record of good works, but it also has a long and sullied record of scandalous sinfulness.

This should not be passed over lightly, as students of history like myself might—"Ah, another episode of corruption; what else is new?" Instead, I need to recall the gravity of the sins and the harm they have done to not merely the reputation of the Church but to thousands upon thousands of men and women, boys and girls. I've never been one for righteous indignation, which for someone like me bleeds over into self-righteousness too easily. But I want more and more to feel deeply a sense of righteous indignation about the Church's mortal sins—most recently, the abuse crisis. On the other hand, when people ask me about becoming Catholic in the wake of this scandal, I have to admit that while I'm deeply disturbed by what has transpired in the name of Christ and his Church, I'm not surprised. I'm not joining an idealized Roman Catholic Church; such a church doesn't exist. I'm joining the Roman Catholic Church as it has been and is. And, among other things, it has been and is horrendously sinful at times.

Aside from corrupt and weak human nature, I can imagine another reason it falls into such sins. Protestant critics who say the Church believes in works righteousness and not in the grace of God have it backwards. If the Church is to be faulted for one thing, it's that it believes too casually in the omnipotent mercy of God. Here's how it works in the confessional. As I confess heinous sins, I worry that I've forfeited the grace of God. At which point, the priest reminds me that to despair of God's forgiveness is itself a sin! That it is the gracious God who makes me feel contrite for my sins; that he has prompted me to come to confession; that he wants me to come to confession because he is a God who loves to bestow mercy.

That gives me courage to continue, after which the priest says, "God, the Father of mercies, through the death and resurrection of his Son has reconciled the world to himself and sent the Holy Spirit among us for the forgiveness of sins; through the ministry of the Church may God give you pardon and peace, and *I absolve you from your sins* in the name of the Father, and of the Son, and of the Holy Spirit" (CCC 1449). The key phrase is "I absolve you." For me this is always an electrifying moment, and I feel viscerally that this is indeed the case. I'm almost tempted to walk away from the sacrament of Reconciliation singing the old fundamentalist song:

Gone, gone, gone, gone, yes my sins are gone.
Jesus has redeemed me and my life's a song.
Buried in the deepest sea,
That is good enough for me,
I shall live eternally,
Praise God, my sins are G-O-N-E gone!

But I'm a good Catholic, and I don't sing fundamentalist songs!

Confession has two requirements: contrition for one's sins ("detestation for the sin committed, together with the resolution not to sin again"

[CCC 1451]) and afterward, penance. Penance is not about "working off" your sins, because it's clear in Catholic teaching that Christ has done that on the cross, and that forgiveness has just been announced by the priest. Here's how the *Catechism* puts it:

> Many sins wrong our neighbor. One must do what is possible in order to repair the harm (e.g., return stolen goods, restore the reputation of someone slandered, pay compensation for injuries). Simple justice requires as much. But sin also injures and weakens the sinner himself, as well as his relationships with God and neighbor. Absolution takes away sin, but it does not remedy all the disorders sin has caused. Raised up from sin, the sinner must still recover his full spiritual health by doing something more to make amends for the sin: he must "make satisfaction for" or "expiate" his sins. This satisfaction is also called "penance." (CCC 1459)

Penance is mostly about engaging in a discipline or act that will help shape me to make amends for sin against neighbors and/or to resist sin in the future.

In my experience, I've not been impressed with priests' attention to the value of penance. Especially after I confess something that I find deeply shameful, the priest will give me a penance of reading a short passage from some saint about God's mercy. I get the point: to avoid despair of God's mercy. I grant that, in the end, that is the greater danger. At other times, I've been told to pray a handful of Hail Marys (not even the complete Rosary, as if I couldn't bear such a penance) or to read a Psalm. I'm sorry to say that this does not cut it if one is interested in growing in Christ. If I have any criticism of contemporary Catholicism as I've experienced it, it's that it believes too casually in the grace of God. I suspect that this is one reason corruption has been a recurring issue in Catholicism; God's mercy is almost taken for granted.

And yet there is another recurring theme in Catholic history, as evidenced by the many, many reform orders and movements that have arisen over the centuries, from the Benedictines to the Franciscans to the Missionaries of

Charity to Word on Fire: the Church never tires of striving to reform itself. Why? That it might live into its holiness in Christ. It's not that the Church's members and leaders do not sin; it's that, in the long run, they refuse to let sin have the last word. Sometimes they justify their evil behavior for decades, but eventually, somebody comes along and says enough is enough. Take Catherine of Siena, who lived during an era especially rife with Church corruption and lax morals. In her famous letter to Pope Gregory XI in February 1376, she wrote,

> I tell you in the name of Christ crucified that you must use your authority. . . . You are in charge of the garden of the holy Church. So [first of all] uproot from that garden the stinking weeds filled of impurity and avarice, and bloated with pride (I mean the evil pastors and administrators who poison and corrupt the garden). . . . Use your authority, you who are in charge of us! Uproot these weeds and throw them out where they will have nothing to administer! Tell them to tend to administering themselves by a good holy life.

The history of the Church is replete with such accusations and pleas. That the Church sins does not impress or depress me. One expects that of fallen human beings. What does impress me is the Church's never tiring effort to reform itself. It is evidence, to me at least, of how seriously the Church takes holiness.

❧

At various times in my journey, I've been intrigued by holiness, and assuming that monks and nuns had a corner on this market, I made vows to live the monastic rhythms, punctuating my life with prayer three, five, or even seven times a day, as well as paying careful attention to the state of my moral life.

This temptation blossomed again as I began seriously contemplating becoming Catholic. Naturally, I wanted to become the Best Catholic Ever. And so I began exploring joining a third order—that is, becoming a Franciscan or Carmelite or Benedictine as a lay person living out my calling in the world. Each order has its own charism, and each has its liturgical practices that one commits to. They all struck me as ways of taking my spiritual life to a new level.

I remember how, in college, I went through a period of being enthralled with the theology of Dietrich Bonhoeffer. I read a passage in one of his books in which he said he'd met a man who wanted to become a saint. Bonhoeffer was gracious, saying that perhaps this man would become a saint. At the time, I thought that this desire was the height of pride and "works righteousness." And after taking up a number of Catholic disciplines like attending daily Mass, reading the daily office, and going to confession, my view was confirmed as I began to recognize the utter selfishness of my desire to become an extraordinary Christian. So one day in confession, I admitted to a priest that I was prideful and wanted to become a saint. He didn't flinch. In fact, he said that was a worthy goal that all of us should strive for. In the meantime, he counseled patience and prudence with matters I was confessing. Catholics really believe in holiness. Catholics believe anyone can, in fact, become a saint. Sometimes when I scan the congregation, especially during daily Mass, I wonder which of those attending will be honored as saints someday.

On the surface, it appears that Catholics believe in two ways of being a Christian, two different paths to follow Christ, two different callings in life for the believer. Some are called, enticed, and even kidnapped by the Spirit into an extraordinary life, like that of the mystics and the monastics. These are said to be Sermon-on-the-Mount Christians who give themselves completely to lives of holiness and devotional intimacy with Christ. I'm thinking of men and women like St. Francis and Dorothy Day, who sought holiness through poverty on the one hand and social justice on the other. And there are those who are starving for a direct encounter with God, and will do whatever it takes to obtain it—fasting, years of renunciation, hours and hours in contemplation before anything comes to fruit. St. Teresa of Avila and St. John of the Cross come to mind, as well as the anonymous author of *The Cloud of Unknowing*. Examples proliferate, to the point that, on many days, the Liturgy of the Hours notes a heroic Christian who was either a mystic, a monastic, or both.

But such men and women are not holy in and for themselves, but are rightly lifted up as inspiration to the rest of us, so that each of us can imitate them in the warp and woof of daily life. They have taken vows of poverty; we, vows of simplicity. They practice sexual abstinence; we, a life of self-control. They commit to obedience to their superiors; we consider the demands of spouse, family, and work as our superiors to whom we owe the obedience of service. But in the end, *both* are driven by the same calling: to be holy as Christ is holy, each in our own capacity and circumstance.

And so, for the Catholic, holiness is something that can be found everywhere, with anyone.

ↄ

And yet there is this paradox in Catholicism: it blesses and celebrates not only the extraordinary life but also the unextraordinary. Catholics drink beer and whiskey. Catholics like parties and festivals. Catholics like to laugh, even at themselves and their Church.

The college group I participated in back in the day was very evangelical in ethos. I remember us debating and then finally deciding that it was okay to have a fellowship event that didn't include prayer, Bible study, or anything particularly religious. This was a hard-fought insight for us. It's a commonplace in Catholic life. I suspect this frustrates Catholics who have had a fresh spiritual awakening. I'd guess that they criticize the Church for having so many raffles and dinners (including dancing!) and the like that get in the way of prayer and devotion. Yes, churches both Protestant and Catholic can become mere social clubs. But in Protestantism, this is a mortal sin. For Catholics, I suspect it's just venial.

That's because the entire Catholic enterprise is grounded in—well, the ground. It is Sacramental with a capital S. The Incarnation is a *big* deal, as is everything related to it. It's why not merely the humanity of the divine Son is celebrated, but also the holiness of the human Mary. It's why physical things—like wood and bones and pieces of metal—can become relics if they have been touched by a saint, another example of holiness in human flesh. It's why geography becomes holy—not just great cities like Jerusalem and Rome, but humble villages like Lourdes, Fatima, and Assisi. In short, nothing in the created order is despised or rejected because everything in the created order can become holy and an object of veneration. And it's why unextraordinary people are accepted for what they aren't, because this is the type of material God likes to work with—broken, imperfect, unholy.

Catholic priests are not surprised or shocked by any sin. A fine literary example is the "whiskey priest" in *The Power and the Glory*. A man was desperately clutching at the priest's ankles, confessing trivial to sordid sins, from enjoying a threesome with two women to not fasting during Lent. The priest's thoughts:

> He had an immense self-importance; he was unable to picture a world of which he was only a typical part—a world of treachery, violence, and lust in which his shame was altogether insignificant. How often the priest had heard the same confession—Man was so limited he hadn't even the ingenuity to invent a new vice: the animals knew as much.

An article on the habitual corruption found in Louisiana politics reveals one side of this paradox. The author describes the moral and psychological shenanigans of Governor Earl Long, brother of the infamous and power-hungry Huey Long. The populace didn't seem to care that, in fact, he'd had an affair with a stripper and landed in a state mental hospital for a spell, as they elected him to the governorship four times in the middle of such scandals:

> The familiar theory . . . was that the people of Louisiana would rather be entertained than served with ethics. Some would call this a Gallic attitude,

to be blinded by charm at the expense of integrity, and indeed the culture of Louisiana is historically French Catholic. And as the Catholics might say, the fall from grace is inevitable, a mystery to be endured rather than a problem to be solved.

This seeming comfortableness with sin is grounded in a profound sense of grace. As the whiskey priest put it, after enduring another typical confession:

> It was for this world that Christ had died; the more evil you saw and heard about you, the greater glory lay around the death. It was too easy to die for what was good or beautiful, for home or children or a civilization—it needed a God to die for the half-hearted and the corrupt.

Catholicism reminds me that I am a member of the fellowship of the half-hearted and corrupt, and that in some ways this is a mystery to be endured in patience rather than solved immediately with prideful, heroic efforts. When the rest of Christendom is ready to cast stones at us for our failures, the Church says, "He who is without sin can cast the first stone." And as we get up from the confessional to make our way back into the world, the same Church says, sometimes rather sternly, "One more thing: Go, and sin no more."

CHAPTER 12

Apostolic

The Catholic Church is apostolic, meaning it is organically and theologically connected with the early Apostles. The current generation of bishops has been ordained by the laying on of hands by the previous generation, and the previous generation by the generation before that, and so on until you arrive at the earliest disciples. The laying on of hands is not merely symbol but a sacrament in which special gifts of the Holy Spirit are given to each new bishop. There is not only an institutional continuity but also a theological one—that is, in what the Church has taught; the Church teaches doctrine that goes back to the Apostles. These points have nuances, but all this has been well argued by others, so I won't spend much time on that here.

As in other chapters in this section, I want to look at how I've witnessed the Church's apostolicity in my journey toward Catholicism—in particular, by looking at my own understanding of some of the Church's ancient teachings.

☙

It may be that apostolicity has been woven into my genes—meaning, I have never really struggled with any core Christian teaching except for a brief period (which I'll describe in a bit). When it comes to the teachings of the Church handed down from the Apostles, and refined and deepened through the centuries, I've had little anxiety. Even though I accepted Christ for selfish and paltry reasons (mainly to relieve guilt during altar calls), it never has occurred to me to question its authenticity. And all through the vagaries of adolescence and the intellectual assault on Christian faith at the very anti-Christian University of California at Santa Cruz, as well as a fair amount of reading in religious skepticism since—well, I've yet to hear a philosophical or psychological argument against Christianity that has had any purchase in my heart and mind.

But there was one season, just a month or so, when I was afflicted with serious doubt, and ironically enough, it took place in seminary. For some reason—certainly not because of anything I was learning in classes—I began to dread dying, and I was troubled with the thought that God may not exist. This came over me not as intellectual wrestling but as just pure existential fear.

And then it passed. I didn't pray or think or psychologize my way out of it. It just left me after a few weeks. I credit the grace of God, or maybe the genes he gave me at birth. From that time to today, I haven't been afraid to die. Yes, I get a little nervous when thinking about it, but it's the type of nervousness I feel before I do something I haven't experienced—like walking into a party of my wife's friends and their spouses. I really don't know anybody there. I'm sure I'll have great conversation with one or two people before the evening is spent. But I admit to a little nervousness as I step into the home. When I think about dying, since I have no idea what happens next exactly, I'm a little anxious. But afraid? No, not really.

This goes along with another faith threat that many people experience today: anger or doubt about the goodness or omnipotence of God in the face of human suffering. I have friends who have had to wrestle with that problem for decades. I intellectually understand the problem, but existentially, it's never troubled me. I have this unwavering belief that God knows what he's doing, and what he's doing is grounded in love and grace. I've come to express this theologically like this: On the cross, we witness a God who is perfectly just and perfectly merciful. Just, in paying the penalty for sin by dying. Merciful, in forgiving all our sin by dying. This God is powerful and loving enough to accomplish this. If the cross is the ultimate revelation of who God is, we can be assured that, despite appearances—it sure looks like God is not loving or in control—that God is indeed continuing to work for the blessedness of

91

humankind. As I said, this is how I work it out intellectually. But I wouldn't be honest if I didn't say that this is first of all an unbidden conviction that rests deep within me. The theology is my attempt to understand why I have unquestioning faith in the goodness and power of God.

If there is one doctrine I sometimes wonder about, it's eternal punishment. I wonder why, if Christ as God died for the sins of all, some would still need to be punished—and for an eternity no less. We're talking about a finite human being with a finite capacity to sin. Eternal punishment overbalances the books, to say the least. One answer to this concern is universalism: there is no hell in the end, but all will enjoy eternal fellowship with God. But when it comes to universalism, to me there is an even greater stumbling block: Jesus. Time and again, he said things that assumed or affirmed a final judgment in which some end up lost forever. One example:

> Very truly, I tell you, the hour is coming, and is now here, when the dead will hear the voice of the Son of God, and those who hear will live. For just as the Father has life in himself, so he has granted the Son also to have life in himself; and he has given him authority to execute judgment, because he is the Son of Man. Do not be astonished at this; for the hour is coming when all who are in their graves will hear his voice and will come out—those who have done good, to the resurrection of life, and those who have done evil, to the resurrection of condemnation. (John 5:25–29)

In Matthew 25 alone, he tells three parables that drive this home: one in which foolish bridesmaids, who failed to prepare for the coming of the bridegroom, are denied entry to the wedding feast, with the bridegroom saying, "I do not know you" (Matt. 25:12); one where a slave who refused to invest the talents the master had given him is punished: "As for this worthless slave, throw him into the outer darkness, where there will be weeping and gnashing of teeth" (Matt. 25:30); and one about those who fail to recognize the Son of Man in the hungry, the naked, and the imprisoned, to which the Son of Man says, "These will go away into eternal punishment" (Matt. 25:46).

Sophisticated exegetes have attempted to subvert the plain meaning of Jesus' words, but for me they've never been convincing. After learning in seminary how to do proper exegesis in the original languages, and after reading hundreds of commentaries about hundreds of passages, I've come to agree with Søren Kierkegaard:

> The matter is quite simple. The Bible is very easy to understand. But we Christians are a bunch of scheming swindlers. We pretend to be unable to understand it because we know very well that the minute we understand we are obliged to act accordingly. Take any words in the New Testament and forget everything except pledging yourself to act accordingly. My God, you will say, if I do that my whole life will be ruined. How would I ever get on in the world? Herein lies the real place of Christian scholarship. Christian scholarship is the Church's prodigious invention to defend itself against the Bible, to ensure that we can continue to be good Christians without the Bible coming too close.

The temptation that universalism dangles before us—and that too much of Protestant Christianity with its empty crosses succumbs to, whether universalist or not—is sentimentalism; that is, it promotes a religion whose main job is to make us feel good about ourselves and about God. To be fair, some American Catholics, in trying to reverse the impression that Catholics teach a religion of suffering, fall prey to this temptation as well. It is a strong temptation in a country characterized by optimism and belief in progress. All in all, the temptation is to leap over the Crucifixion into the Resurrection before the Crucifixion has done its refining work in us. Human beings have a natural desire to feel good—of course! But I've never been convinced that God is mostly interested in making us feel good about ourselves or ensuring that we have an unambiguously positive image of him.

Yes, some biblical passages speak about the comfort and peace that God can give us—thank God! Indeed, comfort and peace are part and parcel of the life of faith. And there is no question that the end of the age is described in terms that highlight our happiness. But when we lock God into the role of comforter of our psychological distress, we are no longer thinking about the biblical God, the real God. That God is also wrapped in mystery; his power and holiness elicit a holy fear in us. As has been said many times, if we imagine that we understand God, if we are more or less comfortable in knowing him and thinking about him—intellectually or emotionally—then we can be sure that we are not thinking about the God and Father of our Lord Jesus Christ. That God is a fearsome God, the one who revealed himself in the "mean and wild" Jesus, whose power and glory when revealed make us both shake in fear and bow in reverence, basking joyfully in his omnipotent mercy.

This is why the greatest symbol of the faith is not a butterfly or even an empty cross but a crucifix. I am thankful that there is one prominently displayed in every Catholic church. My parish, St. Michael's in Wheaton, has a huge crucifix at the front. I can hardly take my eyes off it when I worship. When I wonder where God can be found in the most tragic and unjust suffering imaginable, I find him on the crucifix. When I ponder God's omnipotent mercy to all sinners and sufferers throughout the world, I see it on the crucifix.

The crucifix is not intended to make me feel good as much as to help me know who God is and what he is like. If one were to summarize all the varied strains of Christian doctrine and the paradoxes that abound in the Gospel—if one wants one symbol of apostolicity—to me it is the crucifix.

❧

Upon converting, I was interviewed by many Catholic media outlets, and a question that kept coming up was: "Was there any point of Catholic teaching that you struggled with?" I understand the question; many converts to Catholicism have such a story to tell. But it made no sense to me, for a couple of reasons.

First, as a Christian, I've already "swallowed" a host of outrageous teachings: that the Almighty, Infinite, and Holy God became flesh and lived among us; that he was born of a virgin; that he allowed his holy self to be killed by sinful mortals; that he then turned around and, as a mortal, rose from the dead; that he will return and establish a kingdom on earth; and that, in the meantime, he lives inside me. You think that the Assumption or Immaculate Conception of Mary or transubstantiation are a stumbling block? Theological child's play! Second, I think the question betrays a misunderstanding of faith. For many, faith is more or less something that happens to you. Faith is that feeling or sense of confidence that something you can't *prove* scientifically or logically seems nonetheless true. And thus you find Christians saying, "I believe in this doctrine, but I find it hard to believe in that doctrine." The ultimate judge of the truthfulness of any teaching is then determined by how it impresses me emotionally.

To become a Catholic, one must undergo a shift in how one views reality. Faith in this case is not primarily a warm feeling of confidence—something that occurs in my breast. Faith is not about the feeling inside me as much as something outside the self that I trust—not faith as such but always "faith *in*" something or someone outside me. And it's not the feeling that determines the trust, but the trust that over time shapes my feelings. In short, I am not the one who determines the truth or falsity of any given teaching. Faith is a recognition of one's smallness in the face of teachings that are deeper, wider, and broader than any one mind can comprehend. It's a realization that wisdom lies not in marshaling my puny heart and intellect to determine reality, but in humbly giving myself to something greater than myself and trying to learn from that which is greater.

The Catholic Church claims to be that greater thing—founded by Christ himself and preserved by him throughout the ages, continually guiding the Church into all truth, as he promised (John 16:13). If the Church, then, in its collective wisdom, has said that x is true and y is not, who am I (limited in intellect, emotion, and experience) to mount an assault? Would not the wiser and humbler course be first to try to understand why the Church teaches as it does and ask God to shape my heart and mind around this teaching?

So, yes, having spent over half a century in Protestantism, some Catholic teachings feel uncomfortable—for example, the Immaculate Conception. It's just not something I've ever thought about, and it comes across as strange when first hearing of it. But my approach has been: "Catholics are not stupid. Some great minds have shaped and taught this. What do they see in it? Why do they believe it? How does it accord with other aspects of the faith?" When I explored that briefly, I understood that it did, in fact, have a rather remarkable grounding in Scripture: Mary is described as "full of grace" by the angel Gabriel. In this respect, Catholics are more literal at reading Scripture than are fundamentalists. For Catholics, this means that Mary was conceived and preserved by God's grace fully and completely. It's not that God could not have used a Mary trapped in original sin like the rest of us. But it is fitting that she should be a holy vessel to nurture the Holy One, Jesus, within her. And it's not a matter of Mary earning God's favor and meriting God's grace, because even Mary was saved by the death of her son proleptically—that is, from conception, Mary, too, is saved by Jesus' death and Resurrection. Mary is full of grace because this Jesus died for her too.

Such a doctrine, like all doctrines, cannot be tied up neatly in a bow. Does it satisfy every theological itch I experience when I think about it deeply? Of course not. But not even the Trinity does that: I mean, really, three in one and one in three? No sane human being can sit comfortably with that paradox. But when it comes to the Trinity, the Assumption of Mary, and a host of other teachings, I'm more than happy to live under the umbrella of faith in the Church. The larger point for me is not to stand in judgment deciding whether or not I believe in any particular doctrine, but to humbly give myself to the Church and try to integrate the doctrine into my life and faith. So, to take the Immaculate Conception again, it's not so much a stumbling block as a gateway to a journey to destinations not yet known. And I happen to love travel.

I do not take credit for understanding things this way, because it's always been obvious to me that we are called to give ourselves to something bigger than ourselves. When I was a Presbyterian, I tried to let Presbyterian faith and practice shape my life; the same was true when I become an Anglican. Because to me, the whole point of belonging to something bigger than yourself, like a denomination, was to be shaped by that communion's history, tradition, and ethos.

The mainline, however, has been rudderless theologically for decades, in large part because its leaders believed its tradition and theology too confining. The spirit of the 1950s and 1960s was all about an ecumenism that downplayed the differences that divided us. And thus we had the phenomenon in some churches—to take infant Baptism as an example—in which pastors encouraged parents to decide for themselves whether to baptize or merely dedicate their infants. This has always struck me as a failure of nerve on the part of pastors, as well as bad ecclesiology. It turns the church into a smorgasbord, where people can fashion their faith according to their own lights.

So when I have the opportunity to write about or teach Catholic theology, I don't talk about what I do or don't believe, but about what the Church teaches. I don't have to lie and pretend I've "drunk the Kool-Aid" on every jot and tittle of Catholic teaching. I can say I struggle with this point and that—not so as to protest and rebel as I would in my Protestant days, but to say that I am striving, as a son of the Church, to integrate this teaching into my own heart and mind.

Thus, to me, becoming a Catholic was not about waiting for all my little beliefs and quirks of faith to line up with Catholic theology. That will never happen in this life, because an opinionated person like me has thousands of such quirks. Instead, it's about making a commitment based on, yes, certain fundamental convictions (it is not blind faith, after all), and then letting the Church instruct me in all those areas that might be discomforting to me. To be a Catholic is not as much a matter of immediately and firmly believing everything the Catholic Church teaches, but about being willing to learn, over time, to happily accept and trust it to guide my heart and mind.

CHAPTER 13

Catholic:
Mission

There comes a moment in each of our lives when it first occurs to us that life can be terribly unjust. For me, it was the day I hit my brother.

We were very young; perhaps I was five and he four. We were working a small garden plot on the side of our home in Santa Clara, California. A pleasant sun was bearing down on us on a bright spring day as we planted radish seeds. My dad was gardening nearby, but not paying attention to what we were doing. As we gardened—or really, played in the dirt—my brother Steve became annoyed with me and hit me. Naturally, I hit him back. That's when my father noticed us. I was scolded and ordered to my room.

"But he . . ." I stammered, trying to defend myself.

"You heard what I said," my dad interrupted. "Go to your room. You should not hit your brother."

"But . . ."

"You heard what I said. Go!"

A key part of this story is that my brother was blind. He was one of the ten thousand unfortunate "preemies" who were put in incubators that delivered pure oxygen to help them survive. This was in 1953. One year later, Johns Hopkins ophthalmologist Arnall Patz figured out that this treatment could cause blindness in some. My brother was one of the some. So it wasn't just my brother I was hitting, but a *blind* brother. My father, failing to notice the initial injustice, only saw a fully able child striking a disabled person.

So, at age five, as I lay crying on my bed, my earliest suspicion about justice and truth first emerged. Too young to think this out rationally, I nonetheless sensed something had gone wrong with the world.

❧

The Church is catholic because it is universal, and it is universal in a few different ways (thus my breaking up this mark of the Church into two chapters). The careful reader will also notice that this mark comes last, contra the order in the Nicene Creed, which asserts our faith in the "one, holy, catholic, and apostolic Church." I've put *catholic* last not as a bid to rewrite the Creed, but only to suggest that of all the marks of the Church, this has impressed me the most.

One aspect of the Church's universal character is that it has a universal mission: as the *Catechism* puts it, "The Church is catholic because she has been sent out by Christ on a mission to the whole of the human race" (CCC 831). That mission is to bring light to those in darkness and to rectify, as much as it can in this age, a world gone wrong.

In this regard, two things have most deeply impressed me about Catholicism. The first is the widespread emphasis on the New Evangelization, inaugurated by John Paul II and given continued emphasis by his successors. In his encyclical *Redemptoris Missio*, he describes three missions of the Church:

Mission ad gentes—that is, "to the nations" where "Christ and his Gospel are not known."

Christian communities: "In these communities the Church carries out her activity and pastoral care." This is the ongoing evangelization of those "fervent in the faith."

New Evangelization: "Where entire groups of the baptized have lost a living sense of the faith, or even no longer consider themselves members of the Church, and live a life far removed from Christ and his Gospel. In this case what is needed is a 'new evangelization' or a 're-evangelization.'"

All this warms this former evangelical's heart, for evangelicalism has historically been a movement of spiritual renewal, both in bringing new people to faith and reenergizing the faith of believers.

That is one dimension of the Church's catholicity. The other is demonstrating the Good News in deeds. And here is where the Catholic Church shines—not just in its deeds, which are well known (its hospitals, orphanages, food closets, homeless shelters, and the like), but also in the theology that undergirds its social work, which is often referred to as Catholic social teaching.

Evangelicals, more than most Protestants, have for decades now wrung their hands as they wrestle with how to think about social justice. Liberals are concerned that the church will neglect this, so they often err on the side of making the pursuit of justice everything. Conservatives are worried that it has in fact often become everything, threatening to marginalize the mission to evangelize. What I discovered over time is that when Protestants found themselves stuck trying to articulate a coherent, full-orbed social justice theology, they invariably started quoting Catholic social teaching. That's because Catholics—in papal, conciliar, and episcopal documents—have been articulating a social doctrine for more than a century now, a theology that shows maturity and wisdom, and is imbued with a uniquely Christian ethos.

The richness of these teachings can be understood best through a direct reading of these documents. But one summary, by the United States Conference of Catholic Bishops, is a good place to start. Here are seven key declarations:

> The Catholic Church proclaims that human life is sacred and that the dignity of the human person is the foundation of a moral vision for society.

> How we organize society—in economics and politics, in law and policy —directly affects human dignity and the capacity of individuals to grow in community.

Human dignity can be protected and a healthy community can be achieved only if human rights are protected and responsibilities are met.

A basic moral test is how our most vulnerable members are faring.

Work is . . . a form of continuing participation in God's creation. . . . The basic rights of workers must be respected—the right to productive work, to decent and fair wages, to the organization and joining of unions, to private property, and to economic initiative.

We are one human family whatever our national, racial, ethnic, economic, and ideological differences. We are our brothers' and sisters' keepers, wherever they may be. Loving our neighbor has global dimensions in a shrinking world. At the core of the virtue of solidarity is the pursuit of justice and peace.

We are called to protect people and the planet, living our faith in relationship with all of God's creation. This environmental challenge has fundamental moral and ethical dimensions that cannot be ignored.

To put it another way, the Church seeks to bring justice to those who have been hit by their brother! And more seriously, to attend to the grave tragedies that happen in medicine, law, science, politics—and wherever.

I love Catholic social teaching not only because of its principles, but also because such principles are grounded in something larger than the (understandable) emotional pull to fix a broken world. I refer to the fact that a great deal of social justice work today is driven either by sentimentality or anger. Understandable, as I said, but wholly inadequate to the immense challenges at hand. The Church knows its lifeblood is not guilt or pity or "commitment to the cause," but Jesus himself, especially as he comes to us in prayer and the Eucharist. So there is never any thought of pitting social justice against personal devotion, nor of pitting Catholic social justice warriors against inviting people into a relationship with Jesus Christ. And there is no temptation to retire into private spirituality and an evangelism neglectful of justice, because the Jesus to whom we pray and who comes to us in the concrete substances of bread and wine shapes us to be concerned about the concrete world in which we live and for which Christ died.

Catholics have much less anxiety about these two crucial elements of its universal mission work; they are not in competition but work hand in hand.

CHAPTER 14

Catholic:
Saints

The other aspect of catholicity is the simple, on-the-ground reality of the universal makeup of the Church. Here I refer to the reality that often goes under the heading of *diversity*, which is inadequate to describe what is going on. Our talk about diversity usually ends there. If we see a company that has a healthy balance of men and women, of white, black, Hispanic, and Asian, we usually say, "Isn't it wonderful to see such diversity!" End of conversation. Diversity is an end in itself, with little thought about how it affects unity or integrity or mission, for example, because diversity *is* integrity and mission.

The Catholic Church can partly agree but understands that diversity, if it is to truly contribute to the good, always joins hands with other virtues, especially unity. Otherwise, we often end up with what we have in secular America today: diversity wars, in which minorities are pitted against not only majorities but often against one another, so that unity is sabotaged. That is no better than overemphasizing unity, which will only crush diversity.

I believe the Church holds these virtues in healthy tension—thus the regular example in many congregations in America of services attended by both English and Spanish speakers, or in my church, both whites and Burmese. My Confirmation service at St. Raymond's in Joliet was conducted in both English and Spanish as over half of the confirmands were Hispanic.

More and more Protestant churches are doing this sort of thing, but my sense is that there is usually some self-congratulation hanging in the air. It's as if that church is saying, "Isn't it wonderful how diverse we are!" For Catholics, it's just part and parcel of being "one . . . catholic" Church.

The diversity is important, no question about it, but it is a diversity that is married to a unity, both of which are subservient to something greater than themselves—namely, Jesus Christ. Thus the better term, *catholic* or *universal.*

❦

As a Catholic, you are never allowed to forget that you are not alone, that you enjoy a great diversity of companions in this life below and the one above, and that you all relish the same thing, a something that lies outside the self and outside of your relational dynamics. That "something other" is described in various ways—as the Church, as the life of holiness, as devotion to Christ, as faithfulness to God, and so forth. And on this journey of faith, you have companions to help you along the way.

At every Mass, the priest or deacon announces for whom the Mass is being said. The Mass is in this sense a prayer and an offering for the soul of a pilgrim who continues to make their journey to the fullness of God after this life. Most of us in the service do not know the person for whom the Mass is being said, which to me only highlights the connection we have with the deceased—we are praying for them, just as saints are praying for us. It is a fellowship of prayer shared beyond the boundaries of time and space.

Asking Mary or one of the saints to pray for us is perhaps the most powerful and regular expression of this fellowship. I have no qualms about asking Mary or St. Michael or whomever to pray for me. I am comforted that they pray for me, just as I am comforted when I ask my wife or friends to pray for me. This puzzles many a Protestant, and even some Catholics who spend a lot of time with Protestants. Some ask, "Why ask for the prayers of the saints when you can go directly to God with your concerns?" Well, it's not an either/or. Just as there is a subtle and mysterious power in having many others pray for you, so it is with the saints. The Apostle James said that the prayers of a righteous person have a powerful effect (James 5:16), so it only makes sense that we'd want one of the saints to pray for us.

This question is driven by the assumption that prayer is first and foremost a transaction: we ask and then we receive, if it is God's will. And the more worthy the petitioner, the more likely will the transaction work in one's favor! This sounds base, but there is no question that there are transactions in prayer. Jesus seemed to think that making such requests to our heavenly Father is perfectly appropriate, and that our Father welcomes such prayers. Besides, there is no sense in pretending one doesn't want divine intervention in this matter or that, even if we think it silly or useless.

On the other hand, Jesus clearly teaches that prayer is more than a transaction. What is a more unlikely and useless prayer request (in the near future, anyway) than that God's will be done on earth as it is in heaven, when it's manifestly true, day in and day out, that his will is not done on earth? Obviously, a mere transaction is not at the forefront of prayer for Jesus. That's why some people say, "Prayer is not about changing God but changing us." And of course, there is a large measure of truth in this. If nothing else, in prayer we learn to conform our will to God's will, especially when certain requests seem to be denied year after year. And so we learn patience, forbearance, and hope.

To be fair, even such a notion of prayer is fundamentally about a transaction: we pray so that we can be changed. And if so much of prayer is about one transaction or another, then it makes sense to skip intermediaries and ask to see the Manager, the Man in Charge. And yet, as much as prayer is a transaction, in Catholicism it's first and foremost an expression of friendship: friendship between God and us, and friendship between our diverse brothers and sisters in Christ. If prayer is fellowship—and universal fellowship at that—then it makes perfect sense that we'd want to not only pray to God directly but ask our friends to pray for us as well. And if some of our friends left this life below but live gloriously in the life above, wouldn't it make sense that we'd ask for their prayers too?

‹›

The Litany of Saints, prayed on All Saints Day, at the Easter Vigil, and at Baptisms, is an especially meaningful ritual for me. It was prayed in earlier forms as early as the fifth century, and it is one of only six litanies authorized for use in public services. It is often recited or sung in a shorter form than the one quoted below, which is already a shortened version so as to not test readers' patience. It is prayed alone or in a group setting, with the cantor or priest praying the first line, and the congregation responding:

Lord, have mercy on us. *Christ, have mercy on us.*
Lord, have mercy on us.
Christ, hear us. *Christ, graciously hear us.*
God the Father of heaven, *have mercy on us*
God the Son, Redeemer of the world, *have mercy on us.*
God the Holy Ghost, *have mercy on us.*
Holy Trinity, one God, *have mercy on us.*
Holy Mary, *pray for us* (response repeated after each line below)
Holy Mother of God, ℞.
Holy Virgin of virgins, ℞.
St. Michael, ℞.
St. Gabriel, ℞.
St. Raphael, ℞.
All you holy angels and archangels, ℞.
All you holy orders of blessed spirits, ℞.
St. John the Baptist, ℞.
St. Joseph, ℞.
All you holy patriarchs and prophets, ℞.
St. Peter, ℞.
St. Paul, ℞.
St. Andrew, ℞.
St. James, ℞.
St. John, ℞.
St. Thomas, ℞.

St. James, ℞.

St. Philip, ℞.

St. Bartholomew, ℞.

St. Matthew, ℞.

St. Simon, ℞.

St. Thaddeus, ℞.

St. Matthias, ℞.

St. Barnabas, ℞.

St. Luke, ℞.

St. Mark, ℞.

All you holy apostles and evangelists, ℞.

All you holy disciples of our Lord, ℞.

All you holy innocents, ℞.

St. Stephen, ℞.

St. Lawrence, ℞.

St. Vincent, ℞.

Sts. Fabian and Sebastian, ℞.

Sts. John and Paul, ℞.

Sts. Cosmas and Damian, ℞.

Sts. Gervase and Protase, ℞.

All you holy Martyrs, ℞.

St. Sylvester, ℞.

St. Gregory, ℞.

St. Ambrose, ℞.

St. Augustine, ℞.

St. Jerome, ℞.

St. Mary Magdalene, ℞.

St. Agatha, ℞.

St. Lucy, ℞.

St. Agnes, ℞.

St. Cecilia, ℞.

St. Catherine, ℞.

St. Anastasia, ℞.

All you holy virgins and widows, ℞.

All you holy men and women, saints of God, *intercede for us.*

I quote it at length—and it is longer than this!—to suggest how great is the company of heaven. And we've only listed *some* of the saints up to the Middle Ages.

When it comes to everyday human fellowship, Catholics are as bad as Protestants at being cliquish, at struggling to warmly welcome newcomers, at gossip and prejudice. How one Episcopalian described his church's attitudes toward newcomers applies to Catholics as well in my experience: "We want to give them their space." For an introvert like myself, there is some genius to that. When I enter a new church and am assaulted by an army of warm, smiley greeters (as I am in any evangelical church worth its salt), I'm tempted to do an about-face and run back to my car. I don't want to be noticed, thank you very much, at least for a few Sundays. Every Catholic church I've attended has accommodated my wishes in spades. But I will admit that, overall, the Church as I've experienced it could use a few lessons in welcoming the stranger who shows up in worship.

But if the Catholic Church does not shine in everyday human fellowship, it excels in human fellowship that transcends the everyday. Among other ways that manifests itself is this: everyday Catholics have their saints. They not only have a saint day for every day of the year—and often more than one saint per day—they also spend a lot of time chatting with them. Most Catholics have a favorite saint or two—besides Mary, who is everyone's friend and mother. My wife's aunt, for example, loved St. Joseph and admitted spending more time talking to him than she did with Jesus.

That offends Protestant sensibilities. But think back to the garden. Did it offend God when he found Adam delighting in Eve? Adam doesn't say, "Thank you, God, for giving me this splendid helpmate"; he just marvels at Eve and seems to forget that God is even around. Is God troubled that Adam spends a lot more time hanging around tilling the garden with Eve than spending time with him? It's apparent that sometimes God had to come looking for Adam. And does it really bother God, given all the tasks he's assigned to us and the number of people he calls us to love, that he is not in the forefront of our mind every minute of the day? Sorry, Brother Lawrence, but I'm not convinced that we should "practice the Presence" every waking moment. Instead, we should practice attentiveness to the people and tasks at hand. Could it be that God *wants us* to relish the human life he's created and the fellow human beings he created for us to love and to be loved by? It is hardly a sin to take our troubles to a fellow human being, then, and pour out our hearts to them for hours on end.

The only difference between Protestants and Catholics in this matter is that Catholics do so with friends on earth *and* those in the great company of heaven. And a great and large company it is. The Church's life is littered with saints. And they keep multiplying! According to some estimates, there are over ten thousand canonized Catholic saints. Who can keep track of all of them? Who cares about most of them? St. Augustine, St. Francis, Sts. Teresa of Avila and Thérèse of Lisieux, and the like—yes. But Sts. Narcissus, Argeus, and Marcellinus, who were martyred for refusing Roman military service? Domingo Ibáñez de Erquicia, who was martyred in Japan? Emma of Lesum, who is venerated for good works? Hemma of Gurk, the founder of several churches and monasteries? There are European saints galore, but also saints from Uganda (e.g., Denis Ssebuggwawo Wasswa, martyr), Mexico (e.g., Pedro de Jesús Maldonado Lucero, priest and martyr), Korea (e.g., Anna Pak Agi, martyr), and from every part of the globe. Who cares about such people? Well, even if forgotten today, they were not forgotten by Catholics closer to their day. They are all saints, yes, with a special aura of holiness about them. But they are also friends, people to whom one can bring one's troubles, people who will pray for us, people who remind us that we are not alone in the garden.

And they are people who help us endure the trials of human life. There are saints designated to help with special needs, from the mundane (e.g., St. Anthony, patron saint of stolen or lost things) to the serious (e.g., St. Rita, patron saint of abused women, loneliness, spousal abuse, bad marriages, and widows) to the catastrophic (St. Jude, patron saint of desperate causes). There are saints who help us simply celebrate the life God has given us (e.g., St. Fiacre, patron saint of gardeners; St. Christopher, patron saint of travelers; and of course, St. Frances de Sales, patron saint of writers and journalists!).

That's the thing about the Catholic Church: it embraces humanity—all of it. Not just fellow human beings, but the warp and woof of our common life, from the arts, to sports, to food and drink; it seems nothing is off-limits for Catholics to enjoy. For the Catholic, there is something intrinsically good, true, and beautiful about human existence. And so it's not God alone whom the Catholic Church gives us, but also other men and women whom God made for us. Despite the yearnings of some mystics who conceive the culmination of our journey as being alone with the Alone, the Catholic Church stubbornly insists, and incarnates in its daily life, that the end of the journey is deep fellowship with God *and* with others: to be together with the gathered—all of them in all their diversity.

There is a common prayer at the beginning of Catholic Mass that brings this all together. It suggests the immense diversity of the Church, but a diversity that is not an end in itself but driven by our common yearning to love God with all our thoughts, words, and deeds:

> I confess to almighty God
> and to you, my brothers and sisters,
> that I have greatly sinned,
> in my thoughts and in my words,
> in what I have done and in what I have failed to do,
> through my fault, through my fault,
> through my most grievous fault;
> therefore I ask blessed Mary ever-Virgin,
> and all the Angels and Saints,

and you, my brothers and sisters,
to pray for me to the Lord our God.

Here is God. Here are my brothers and sisters. Here is Mary ever-Virgin, as well as all the angels and saints—that wild diversity of love, all engaged in praying with one another that we might ever more deeply love God and neighbor.

That's what I call a catholic Catholic prayer.

CHAPTER 15

All Together, Now and Forever

Besides formal beliefs, there are psychological/intellectual shifts one must undergo in order to become a Catholic. Or at least it was so for me. I've talked about the shift from a belief in primitivism to a trust in tradition, and from acting as theological judge and jury to submitting to something greater than myself. There is one more shift worth mentioning before I conclude.

The longer I traveled in evangelicalism, the more suspicious I became of what is traditionally called "enthusiasm"—that is, a faith that is driven by emotion. In my experience, one of the things that increasingly troubled me about the evangelical movement was how dependent it was on emotion. For evangelicals, the spontaneous and the emotive are true signs of religious authenticity. Formal written prayers may be helpful in some ways, but when one wants to really get down with God, nothing but spontaneous expressions will do. And though duty and ritual play a role in the life of some evangelicals, like Anglicans, it's usually emotion that still signals the sincerity of one's faith.

Thus the evangelical tradition of revivals; the evangelical style of preaching, which is earnest and heartfelt and spoken without a manuscript; the importance of conversational prayer, in which we pour out our hearts to God as we would a friend; the understanding of faith as a heartfelt and warm sense of conviction; the contemporary evangelical worship service, in which praise choruses dominate, and in which the service is designed to end on an emotional upbeat. And both revivals and megachurch worship speak to the evangelical habit of wanting to do things big, with lots of people, because in such settings, emotions can be employed to their best.

I recently spoke with a friend deeply attracted to Catholicism. But he said he found that, in terms of emotional engagement, Catholic services paled in comparison to his Anglican charismatic church. That church's service moves forward into an emotional pitch in the many praise songs that are pieced together after communion. The service is clearly designed to be a mini-revival week after week. He said he would miss that if he became a Catholic. My friend assumes that true religion is an emotive religion. For evangelicals, emotion is the outward sign of an inward grace. Without it, you're not sure if you are a real Christian. Or, to put it another way, emotion is a kind of sacrament for many evangelicals.

Now, there is something to be said for this: a faith that has no emotional texture is likely not faith in Jesus Christ, in the forgiveness of sins, in the life everlasting. Thus the pleasant surprise of Catholics who discover this when they attend an evangelical church. On the other hand, to equate the sincerity and depth of one's faith with emotions that lie on the surface of the heart—well, that's a problem in my view.

It is true, certainly in my experience, that Catholic Mass is much less exuberant and emotion-laden than a typical evangelical service. But that is not a bug but a feature of Catholic worship. The center of Catholic worship is not an emotional moment taking place inside the heart and mind but the re-presentation of the death of Christ on the altar, and the concrete reception of his Body and Blood. It does not matter how one feels at that moment; what matters is that one is communing with Christ bodily and spiritually. And thus the Mass is not designed to get one into an emotional state, but to prepare one to receive Christ and then serve him in the world. To move out of evangelicalism and into Catholicism, one must abandon the idea that true religion is about sustaining the emotion it sometimes generates inside us; instead, it is about an act that the Church does apart from one's emotional state—the sacrifice of the Eucharist and our reception of it.

This is why liturgical prayers are more essential to Catholic religion than spontaneous praying. It's a great thing when anyone, including Catholics, learns how to pray to God in personal language from the heart, no matter how clumsy it may sound. I also think it is a good practice to learn how to pray aloud in front of others in this way. But it is certainly not the case that spontaneous speech is authentic and written speech is not. I for one have blurted out too many things over my lifetime that have caused grief and embarrassment. In most cases, I simply didn't mean what I said. My words were inauthentic—not matching what I was really thinking or what I meant to say. On the other hand, can one really argue that the Gettysburg Address failed to express authentically what Abraham Lincoln was thinking and believing?

Of course, the spontaneous utterance can be authentic, just as the written speech can be phony. Still, Catholicism privileges ritual over the spontaneous and does so precisely to protect the faith from being overtaken by emotion, to keep the faith focused not on what goes on inside the human breast, but on what God has done for us and to us in Christ. You can't become Catholic until you make this shift. Well, at least I couldn't.

છ

Naturally, I'm not arguing that there is no role for emotion in the life of faith; I'm concerned only when religious leaders try to manufacture religious sentiment week in and week out in an attempt to keep the faithful—well, faithful.

That being said, genuine religious faith will from time to time enjoy arresting events that deeply move both mind and heart. One such moment happened twenty-five years before I was confirmed, and looking back, I believe it planted me in the strong current that would sweep me up and take me to Rome.

In the 1990s, I was in that grand city helping lead a *Christian History* tour focusing on the history of the early Church. We left open one day in Rome for participants to explore the city as they wished. It happened to be a Wednesday, when Pope John Paul II gave a weekly address to pilgrims in St. Peter's Square. I decided to see what it was about. As I arrived in the square, two things immediately impressed me. First was the architecture. The square, created between 1656 and 1667 at the hand of Gian Lorenzo Bernini, is over three football fields long and two wide. In an ellipse around the piazza, he built massive Doric columns four deep, on top of which his disciples later put statues of 140 saints. With the saints looking down from atop the huge elliptical columns, one cannot help but feel embraced, in the words of Bernini, with "the maternal arms of Mother Church."

I arrived early for the general audience, but already the square was filled with pilgrims, perhaps ten thousand or so, many of whom had come in groups from all over the world—black, Hispanic, Asian, and Caucasian. Praise songs and choruses in Portuguese, French, Spanish, Italian, and English punctuated the quiet whispers and prayers of anticipation of the pope's arrival. When he did arrive, the excited pilgrims cheered and waved. He drove around a roped-off section of the piazza in the center, waving in return to us. Perhaps everyone there had the same experience as did I: I was only seven deep as he drove by, and I'm sure a smiling Pope John Paul II looked me directly in the eye with a subliminal personal greeting! He then mounted a podium and gave an address in a least four or five languages.

I do not remember a thing he said, in part because I was stunned with the grandeur of the moment. It was not the architecture or the pilgrims' enthusiasm or the pope's charisma; given who I am, it was the theology—more particularly, the ecclesiology—that impressed me almost mystically.

Here I was witnessing the one, holy, apostolic, and catholic Church. No other Christian tradition has a place at which and a person around whom the whole Church can gather and celebrate God's goodness to us in Christ. As I've said, I understand that, ultimately, the Church's four attributes are grounded in Christ: the Church is one because Christ is one; it is holy because Christ is holy; it is catholic because Christ is catholic; and it is apostolic because Christ is apostolic. Even when Catholics fail to display one or more of these attributes—and there is no shortage of examples of that!—the Church is still one, holy, catholic, and apostolic because of Christ's identification and unity with his Church. But again, metaphysical theology is not my interest here; practical theology is.

At St. Peter's, I witnessed the one Church, gathered in one place, around one person, who for Catholics is the representative not only of Peter but the

Lord Jesus, who gave to Peter the very keys to the kingdom; the holy Church, as symbolized by the 140 saints who looked down on us, men and women known and obscure—from Theodora, Galla, Vitus, and Marcellinus to Jerome, Athanasius, Francis Xavier, and Thomas Aquinas—whose lives were shaped by the love and holiness of Christ; the apostolic Church, represented most powerfully in the teaching office of the pope, who exhorted the faithful that day as he did every Wednesday, not to mention in other addresses and encyclicals.

On that sunny, summer morning in St. Peter's Square, I experienced a reality, a mode of existence that bursts upon us ever so briefly now and then. The Catholic Church—from every tribe and tongue, nation and ethnicity, from the four corners of the earth—gathered not only to celebrate the Church's unity, but also, in song especially, the Church's diversity; not only its holiness but also its apostolicity. It was indeed an emotion-laden event for me, but what remains is not what was happening inside me, but what was happening outside of me, something greater and grander than the self. And though it would take a few more years to see where this led, I eventually found myself at home, with all the company of heaven and earth.

NOTES

18–19   **In the heart of every Christian**: John Paul II, *The Splendor of Truth* 117, encyclical letter, August 6, 1993 (Washington, DC: United States Conference of Catholic Bishops, 1993), 173–174.

19–20   **A messenger comes and says**: *St. Francis of Assisi: Writings and Early Biographies: English Omnibus of the Sources for the Life of St. Francis*, 4th rev. ed., ed. Marion A. Habig, trans. Raphael Brown et al. (Bangalore: Asian Trading, 1983), 1501–1502. Quoted in "Francis of Assisi," *Christian History* 42, vol. 13, no. 2 (1994): 21.

25   **Most merciful God**: *The Book of Common Prayer: And Administration of the Sacraments and Other Rites and Ceremonies of the Church Together with the Psalter or Psalms of David* (New York: Church Publishing, 2007), 79.

25–26   **Almighty God, Father of all Mercies**: *The Book of Common Prayer: And Administration of the Sacraments and Other Rites and Ceremonies of the Church Together with the Psalter or Psalms of David* (New York: Church Publishing, 2007), 101.

28   **Among other things, he denied the deity of Jesus Christ**: Wikipedia's "John Shelby Spong" entry, Wikimedia Foundation, last modified July 14, 2021, https://en.wikipedia.org/wiki/John_Shelby_Spong.

30   **I wrote a book to just this end**: Mark Galli, *Beyond Smells & Bells: The Wonder and Power of Christian Liturgy* (Brewster, MA: Paraclete, 2008).

46   **When asked how we are doing**: David Zahl, "500 Years After Luther, We Still Feel the Pressure to Be Justified," *Christianity Today,* December 30, 2016, https://www.christianitytoday.com/ct/2017/january-february/pressure-to-be-justified.html.

47   **Sanctification . . . is perhaps best defined**: Gerhard O. Forde, "The Lutheran View," in *Christian Spirituality: Five Views of Sanctification,* ed. Donald L. Alexander (Downers Grove, IL: IVP Academic, 1988), 13–32, at 13.

47   **a biography of Barth**: Mark Galli, *Karl Barth: An Introductory Biography for Evangelicals* (Grand Rapids, MI: Eerdmans, 2017).

47   **The divine pardon**: Karl Barth, *Church Dogmatics*, vol. 4, *The Doctrine of Reconciliation,* Part 1, ed. G.W. Bromiley and T.F. Torrance (Edinburgh: T&T Clark, 1956), 576.

49   **In faith we together hold the conviction**: *Joint Declaration on the Doctrine of Justification by the Lutheran World Federation and the Catholic Church* 15 (1999), https://www.lutheranworld.org/jddj.

49   **O Great Merciful God**: Maria Faustina Kowalska, *Diary of Saint Maria Faustina Kowalska: Divine Mercy in My Soul* 1570 (Stockbridge, MA: Marian Press, 2005), 345.

49–50   **According to Catholic understanding**: *Joint Declaration on the Doctrine of Justification by the Lutheran World Federation and the Catholic Church* 38 (1999), https://www.lutheranworld.org/jddj.

53   **The liturgical services of the church**: Mother Raphaela, *Living in Christ: Essays on the Christian Life by an Orthodox Nun* (Crestwood, NY: St. Vladimir's Seminary, 1998), 17.

54   **We complain that He does not make Himself present**: Anthony Bloom, *Beginning to Pray* (Mahwah, NJ: Paulist, 1970), 26.

60   **"how God uses Catholicism to utter his Word"**: Robert Barron, *Catholicism: A Journey to the Heart of the Faith* (New York: Image Books, 2011), 278.

60   **For I am certain that God speaks**: Robert Barron, *Catholicism: A Journey to the Heart of the Faith* (New York: Image Books, 2011), 278–279.

63   ***When Did We Start Forgetting God?***: Mark Galli, *When Did We Start Forgetting God? The Root of the Evangelical Crisis and Hope for the Future* (Carol Stream, IL: Tyndale Momentum, 2020).

76   **Let us rejoice then and give thanks**: Augustine, *In Joannis evangelium* (PL 35:1568). Quoted in English in CCC 795.

76   **"About Jesus Christ and the Church"**: *Acts of the Trial of Joan of Arc*. Quoted in English in CCC 795.

78   **"When God touches man's heart"**: Council of Trent, *Decree on Justification* 5, in *Compendium of Creeds, Definitions, and Declarations on Matters of Faith and Morals*, ed. Heinrich Denzinger et al. (San Francisco: Ignatius Press, 2012), 1525, 276.

85   **I tell you in the name of Christ crucified**: Catherine of Siena, Letter T206/G5/DT63, in *The Letters of Catherine of Siena*, vol. 2, ed. Suzanne Noffke (Tempe, AZ: Arizona Center for Medieval and Renaissance Studies, 2001), 61.

88   **He had an immense self-importance**: Graham Greene, *The Power and the Glory* (New York: Penguin Books, 1962), 97.

88–89 **The familiar theory . . . was that the people of Louisiana**: Nancy Lemann, "Exquisite Scandal: Disgrace Comes in Various Forms. Some Are Better Than Others," *Lapham's Quarterly* 13, no. 2 (Spring 2020), https://www.laphamsquarterly.org/scandal/exquisite-scandal.

89   **It was for this world that Christ had died**: Graham Greene, *The Power and the Glory* (New York: Penguin Books, 1962), 97.

93   **The matter is quite simple**: Søren Kierkegaard, "Kill the Commentators," in *Provocations: Spiritual Writing of Kierkegaard*, comp. and ed. Charles E. Moore (Walden, NY: Plough, 1999), 201.

99   ***Mission ad gentes*—that is, "to the nations"**: John Paul II, *Redemptoris Missio* 1 (December 7, 1990), Vatican.va.

99   **"In these communities the Church carries out her activity"**: John Paul II, *Redemptoris Missio* 33 (December 7, 1990), Vatican.va.

99   **"Where entire groups of the baptized"**: John Paul II, *Redemptoris Missio* 33 (December 7, 1990), Vatican.va.

100–101 **The Catholic Church proclaims**: United States Conference of Catholic Bishops, "Seven Themes of Catholic Social Teaching," https://www.usccb.org/beliefs-and-teachings/what-we-believe/catholic-social-teaching/seven-themes-of-catholic-social-teaching.

110–111   **I confess to almighty God**: "Formula of General Confession," in *The Roman Missal* (Washington, DC: International Commission on English in the Liturgy, 2010), 515.

114   **The square, created between 1656 and 1667**: See Wikipedia's "St. Peter's Square" entry, Wikimedia Foundation, last modified July 31, 2021, https://en.wikipedia.org/wiki/St._Peter%27s_Square; "St. Peter's Square," Civitatis Rome, https://www.rome.net/st-peters-square.